PowerPoint® 2003
Just the Steps™
FOR
DUMMIES®

by Barbara Obermeier &
Ted Padova

WILEY

Wiley Publishing, Inc.

PowerPoint® 2003 Just the Steps™ For Dummies®

Published by
Wiley Publishing, Inc.
111 River Street
Hoboken, NJ 07030-5774
www.wiley.com

WILEY

About the Authors

Barbara Obermeier is principal of Obermeier Design, a graphic design studio in Ventura, California. She's the author of *Photoshop CS2 All-in-One Desk Reference For Dummies* and has contributed as author, coauthor, or technical editor on numerous books. Barb is also a faculty member in the Visual Communication Department at Brooks Institute.

Ted Padova is the author of over 20 computer books. He writes primarily on Adobe Acrobat, Adobe Photoshop, Photoshop Elements, and Adobe Illustrator. He is a nationally and internationally known speaker on Adobe Acrobat and digital imaging.

Dedications

I would like to dedicate this book to Gary, Kylie, and Lucky.

—Barbara Obermeier

For Arnie

—Ted Padova

Authors' Acknowledgments

We would like to thank our project editor, Paul Levesque, who kept the book on track; Bob Woerner, our excellent Sr. Acquisitions Editor at Wiley Publishing; Marvin Hoffman, an accomplished technical editor; Andy Hollandbeck, who refined our writing; and the dedicated production staff at Wiley Publishing.

Publisher's Acknowledgments

We're proud of this book; please send us your comments through our online registration form located at `www.dummies.com/register/`. Some of the people who helped bring this book to market include the following:

Acquisitions, Editorial, and Media Development

Project Editor: Paul Levesque

Sr. Acquisitions Editor: Bob Woerner

Copy Editor: Andy Hollandbeck

Technical Editor: Marvin Hoffman

Editorial Manager: Leah P. Cameron

Media Development Manager: Laura VanWinkle

Editorial Assistant: Amanda Foxworth

Cartoons: Rich Tennant (`www.the5thwave.com`)

Composition Services

Project Coordinator: Adrienne Martinez

Layout and Graphics: Denny Hager, Joyce Haughey, Lynsey Osborn, Melanee Prendergast, Heather Ryan

Proofreaders: Jessica Kramer, Joe Niesen, Sossity R. Smith

Indexer: Glassman Indexing Services

Publishing and Editorial for Technology Dummies

Richard Swadley, Vice President and Executive Group Publisher

Andy Cummings, Vice President and Publisher

Mary Bednarek, Executive Acquisitions Director

Mary C. Corder, Editorial Director

Publishing for Consumer Dummies

Diane Graves Steele, Vice President and Publisher

Joyce Pepple, Acquisitions Director

Composition Services

Gerry Fahey, Vice President of Production Services

Debbie Stailey, Director of Composition Services

Contents at a Glance

Table of Contents

*W*elcome to Microsoft PowerPoint 2003. This industry-leading program has an abundance of tools and commands to satisfy all your presentation needs. Whether you want to present important material to your colleagues or clients or just show off your latest travel photos, *Microsoft PowerPoint 2003 Just the Steps For Dummies* has something for you.

About This Book

This book cuts all the fluff out of a computer book and takes you right to steps to produce an effect, task, or job. The book is not linear. However, in some cases, you might need to move around a little to understand one concept before moving to another. Each series of steps is defined with headings to simplify your task of searching for a specific item and finding similar tasks related to a particular concept. Be certain to look back at the Table of Contents when you aren't certain where to find one task or another.

Whenever you want to get something done with this book, try to discipline yourself to follow this method:

1. **Pick the task.** Glance over the Table of Contents to find a category you want to explore — something like working with pictures, which we cover in Chapter 9.

2. **Find it fast.** This is easy because the chapters are designed with coverage of similar items within each chapter. Look over the subheadings listed in the Table of Contents to find a specific task within a given chapter.

3. **Get it done.** Mimic each step and look at the accompanying figures to help you thoroughly understand a given task.

Why You Need This Book

Microsoft PowerPoint 2003 is one of those programs that many people need and use, but they often know just enough to get by. What happens when you want to implement something you haven't used before, like hyperlinks or sound? Most programs today don't come with written documentation

Introduction

Conventions used in this book

➡ We use the ⇨ symbol for menu commands. This tells you to follow the path to select a menu command. Something like "Choose Format⇨Background" is our way of saying "Choose Background from the Format menu." When you select this particular menu command, the Background dialog box opens.

➡ Web site addresses appear in a monospace font to make them easy to identify — for example — `www.dummies.com`. Type the URL in your Web browser's Location bar exactly as you see the monospace type.

➡ To help clarify steps, some figures contain a circle or callout symbol. Look carefully at each figure to fully understand what we're talking about in the text.

 Look for this icon to find tips, notes, and special points of interest throughout the text.

anymore. You'll probably have to search through skimpy online Help files or, worse, wade through lots of tedious narrative text in a gigantic reference manual to find the help you need.

This book eliminates background descriptions and detailed explanations and takes you directly to a series of steps to produce precisely what you want to do with a presentation. If you want it simple, fast, and direct, then this is the book for you.

How This Book Is Organized

This book is organized into four parts. The following sections introduce each one.

Part 1: Creating a Presentation

If you are fairly new to PowerPoint, the chapters in this part get you up and running. First, you find out how to create a presentation. After your presentation is started, we show you how to add content from scratch, from Word, and from existing presentations. You then find the necessary steps on how to edit and format your content to get just the look you want. We finish this part by giving you information on working with the various types of masters in PowerPoint.

Part 11: Adding Visual Interest to Slides

After you have a basic presentation, you may want to add elements to increase visual interest. These comprehensive chapters show you how to do just that. You find out how to add and edit simple graphics like shapes, lines, and arrows. You then find steps on how to add shadows and 3-D effects to those shapes and also to text. If that isn't enough, you discover how to jazz up your text by using the WordArt feature. We also give you all the steps you need to know on how to apply color, texture, and

pattern to your slide elements. Pictures score big with added visual punch. We show you how to bring in both clip art and photos to your presentations. Finally, we round out this part by giving you all you need to create and fully edit tables, graphs, organizational charts, and diagrams.

Part 111: Adding a Dash of Pizzazz with Multimedia

If text, shapes, and pictures aren't enough for you, you may want to explore using sound, movies, and animation in your presentations. It isn't nearly as complicated as you might think. We give you the steps to insert sound and movie files from various sources. You also find out how to use hyperlinks to jump to other slides and presentations or to a Web site. To make your presentation flow smoothly, we show you how to implement transitions between your slides. And lastly, to make your presentation really come alive, you find steps on animating slides, objects, and text.

Part 1V: Presenting Effectively

When your presentation is ready, we show you how to prepare and share it with the world. You find important information on setting up your show options for optimum performance. We give you the steps on printing your slides, handouts, and notes for your audience. You find out how to package your presentation on CD and how to hold an online presentation meeting. Finally, you discover how to give a presentation live, via a kiosk, or over the Web.

Get Ready To

Glance over the Table of Contents to locate the task you want to perform in Microsoft PowerPoint. You don't need to grasp any background information; just jump into the series of steps that defines a solution for a project you want to complete.

Part I
Creating A Presentation

Getting Started with PowerPoint

*T*he first step of any journey through Microsoft PowerPoint is to start up the program and either a) create a new presentation or b) open an existing presentation. Obviously, you can't do anything in PowerPoint until you launch the program.

In this chapter, we talk about some methods you can use to launch PowerPoint and how you can immediately begin to create a new presentation. We also show you how to save a presentation after you've created it and safely exit the program.

Note that, at this point, we assume you have installed either the entire Microsoft Office 2003 suite or just Microsoft Office PowerPoint 2003. If you need to perform an installation, refer to the user documentation accompanying your installer CD for installation instructions.

Chapter 1

Get ready to . . .

Start PowerPoint Using the Start Menu

1. Start your computer and log on to Windows if your computer is not on.

2. Choose Start Menu⇨Programs⇨Microsoft Office⇨ Microsoft PowerPoint 2003 (see Figure 1-1). Microsoft PowerPoint opens, and you're ready to create a new slide presentation or open an existing presentation.

Start PowerPoint Using Keyboard Shortcuts

1. Hold the Ctrl key down and press Esc.

2. Press the P key on your keyboard to select Programs.

3. Press right, left, up, and down arrows to navigate through the menu commands and folders until you arrive at Microsoft PowerPoint 2003.

4. Press Enter to launch PowerPoint (as shown in Figure 1-2).

 You can also create a program shortcut on your desktop. Locate Microsoft PowerPoint 2003 on your Start menu and right-click the PowerPoint application icon to open a context menu. Choose Send To⇨Desktop (create shortcut). The program shortcut is created on your desktop. Just double-click the shortcut icon and PowerPoint launches.

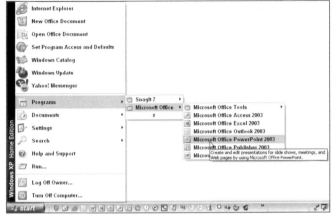
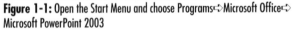

Figure 1-1: Open the Start Menu and choose Programs⇨Microsoft Office⇨ Microsoft PowerPoint 2003

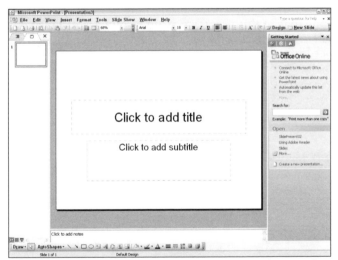

Figure 1-2: Click Microsoft PowerPoint 2003 on the Start menu or select Microsoft PowerPoint 2003 and press Enter to open the program

Open a Saved Presentation

1. Launch PowerPoint.

2. Choose File➪Open and the Open dialog box appears (see Figure 1-3). Alternately, you can press Ctrl+O to open the Open dialog box.

3. Using the Look In drop-down menu, navigate to your hard drive and locate the folder where you have a saved presentation.

4. Choose List from the View drop-down menu to display slide presentations in a list.

5. Click a presentation to select it.

 If you want to open multiple presentations, press the Ctrl key and click each presentation you want to open in the Open dialog box. Click Open and PowerPoint opens all the selected presentations.

6. Click Open and the presentation opens in PowerPoint.

Close a Presentation

1. Open a PowerPoint document in PowerPoint.

2. Click the X in the top-right corner of the PowerPoint Document window (see Figure 1-4). Be certain to click the X appearing in the top-right corner of the Document window. Another X appears at the top-right corner of the PowerPoint application window. If you click this X, the program quits.

 Alternately, you can choose File➪Close to close the document. After closing a file, PowerPoint remains open and ready for you to create a new presentation or open another presentation.

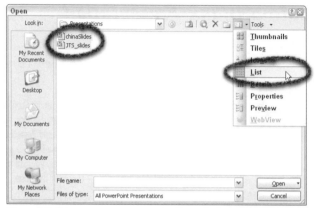

Figure 1-3: Select one or more presentation files in the Open dialog box and click Open

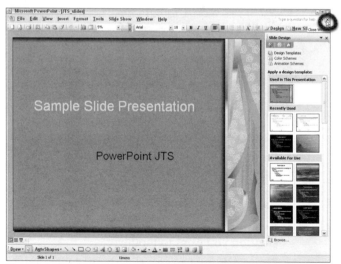

Figure 1-4: Click the X in the top-right corner of the Document window or choose File➪ Close to close the open document

Create a Blank Presentation

1. Open PowerPoint.

2. Click Getting Started in the Task pane to open a drop-down menu.

 The Task pane at the right side of the PowerPoint window contains several panes with menus to assist you in creating and editing slide presentations. If the pane is not visible when you open PowerPoint or you accidentally lose the pane, choose View⇨Task Pane or press Ctrl+F1. If you need more room to view your slides, you can close the pane by clicking the X in the top-right corner of the pane.

3. Select New Presentation from the menu (see Figure 1-5).

 By default, PowerPoint opens a new blank presentation document when you launch the program. If you want to begin working on a new presentation, you can start with the document appearing on program launch. You can also use any of these options to create a new blank document: click Getting Started and select New Presentation, choose File⇨New, click the New button on the toolbar, or press Ctrl+N. You can use any of these options to create a new blank document.

4. In the New Presentation task pane (see Figure 1-6), select one of the following options to create a presentation:

- **Blank Presentation:** Create a new blank presentation.

- **From Design Template:** Use one of the many design templates installed with PowerPoint.

- **From AutoContent Wizard:** The AutoContent Wizard helps you with presentation ideas.

- **From Existing Presentation:** Open an existing presentation you want to modify.

- **Photo Album:** Create a slideshow of pictures.

5. To create a blank presentation, click the Blank Presentation option in the New Presentation Task pane.

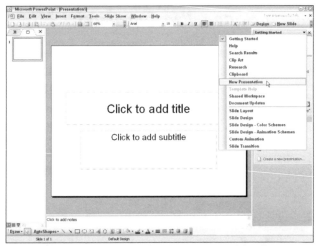

Figure 1-5: Select New Presentation from the Getting Started drop-down menu

Figure 1-6: Click Blank Presentation in the New Presentation Task pane to create a new blank presentation

Create a Presentation Based on a Template

1. Open PowerPoint.

2. Click Getting Started in the Task pane to open the drop-down menu.

3. Select New Presentation.

4. Click From Design Template to open the Slide Design task pane (see Figure 1-7).

5. Scroll the Slide Design Task pane by dragging the slider on the right side of the pane up and down to view all templates. You have slides organized into three separate categories in the Slide Design pane. The categories include

   Used in this Presentation: Any design templates used in the open PowerPoint document appear in this category.

   Recently Used: Templates you have used in recent PowerPoint projects conveniently appear in this category.

   Available for Use: This category contains all the design templates available to you for creating new presentations.

6. Select the template you want to use in a new presentation from the *Available for Use* category (as shown in Figure 1-8).

 Note that the template you select in the Slide Design Task pane shows you a view of the opening slide called the *title slide*. The title slide design is usually different from the presentation slides. When you add additional slides to your presentation, the slide design used for the presentation slides is similar to the title slide but not identical.

Figure 1-7: Click From Design Template in the New Presentation Task pane to open the Slide Design Task pane

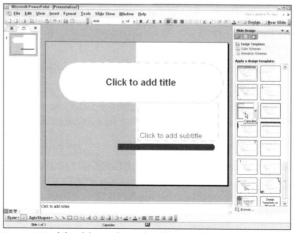

Figure 1-8: Click a slide template in the Slide Design Task pane

Create a Presentation Using the AutoContent Wizard

1. In PowerPoint, click Getting Started to open the drop-down menu.

2. Select New Presentation from the menu.

3. Click From AutoContent Wizard.

4. The AutoContent Wizard opens. In the opening pane, click Next and you arrive at the second pane (see Figure 1-9).

5. Click a category from one of the following:

   - **All:** Lists all slide presentations in all categories. You can scroll the window and select a slide presentation to create from the list.

   - **General:** Displays a list of general business topics.

   - **Corporate:** Displays a list of corporate topics such as business plans, financial reports, employee orientation, and so on.

   - **Projects:** Lists presentations that might be used in a planning process.

   - **Sales/Marketing:** Lists presentations suited for a marketing program.

6. Click a presentation from within a category and click Next to move to the next pane (see Figure 1-10).

7. Select an output option from one of the following:

   - **On-Screen Presentation:** Click this radio button to create a presentation that is intended to be shown on your computer or on a projector connected to your computer.

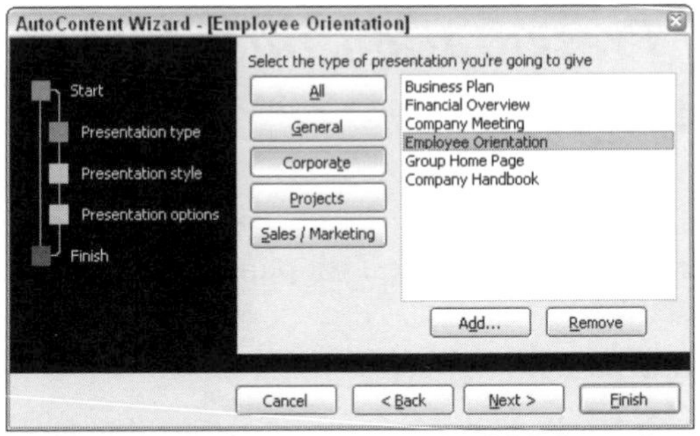

Figure 1-9: Open the AutoContent Wizard and click the Next button to arrive at the second pane

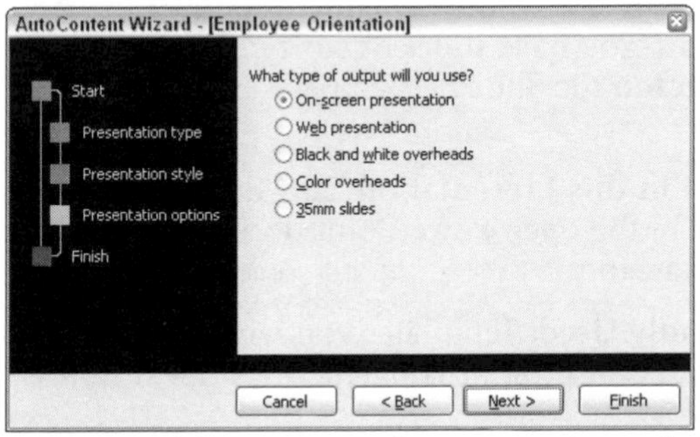

Figure 1-10: Click Next to move to the next pane in the wizard

- **Web Presentation:** Click this radio button for a slide presentation that you want to show on a Web site.

- **Black and White Overheads:** Click this radio button if you want to print your slides on clear acetate on a black-and-white laser printer.

- **Color Overheads:** Click this radio button if you want to print your slides on clear acetate on a color printer.

- **35mm Slides:** Click this radio button if you want to print your slides on a commercial film recorder that outputs to 35mm slides.

8. Click Next to advance to the next pane (see Figure 1-11).

9. Type a title for your presentation in the Presentation Title text box.

10. Type a footer in the Footer text box if you want a footer to appear on your slides.

By default, the date of the last update and the slide numbers will appear on the new presentation. If you don't want such information to appear on the slides, uncheck the respective check box in the wizard.

11. Click Next in the wizard to advance to the last pane in the wizard.

12. Click Finish to complete the slide creation and open it in PowerPoint (see Figure 1-12).

13. Edit the presentation to customize it for your own needs.

The slide presentation opens in Normal view with the Outline tab in view. You can edit text in the Outline tab or directly on each slide to change text and customize the presentation for your own use.

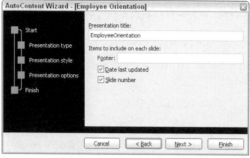

Figure 1-11: Click Next to open the next pane in the wizard, where you type a name for your presentation

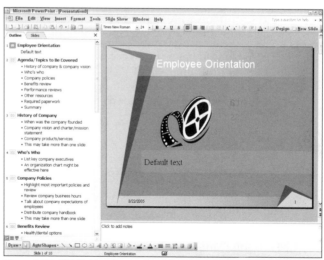

Figure 1-12: Click Finish in the wizard and the new presentation opens in PowerPoint

Change the Opening Default View

1. Open PowerPoint and choose Tools⇨Options.

2. Click the View tab in the Options dialog box (see Figure 1-13).

3. Uncheck the Startup Task Pane option.

 When you remove the check mark for the Startup task pane, PowerPoint opens with the Task pane closed and provides you more viewing and editing room when working on slides. Press Ctrl+F1 to show the Task pane.

4. Review other options on the View tab. You can make choices for items to remain in view or toggle off the views for the Show and Slide Show options.

5. Select the option you want to see when you launch PowerPoint from the Default View drop-down menu. The default option is The View Saved in the File, which shows you the last view when you saved your file in PowerPoint.

Change Save Options

1. Open PowerPoint and choose Tools⇨Options.

2. Click the Save tab in the Options dialog box (see Figure 1-14).

3. Type a default directory path — pointing to the place where you want PowerPoint to save your presentation files — into the Default File Location text box. The default folder is My Documents.

4. Click OK in the Options dialog box.

Figure 1-13: Remove the Startup task pane check mark to provide more viewing and editing room when working on slides

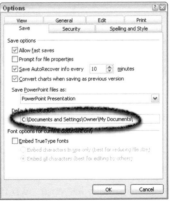

Figure 1-14: Typing in a new directory path for where you want to save your PowerPoint slides

 Look over other options on the Save tab and adjust settings according to your personal needs. Click each tab in the Options dialog box and you can customize PowerPoint to suit your personal work habits. When you need information on given settings in the tabs, consult the PowerPoint Help document (choose Help⇨Microsoft Office PowerPoint Help).

Save a Presentation

1. Create a new blank presentation or a presentation from a design template.

2. Open the File menu and select one of the following:

   - **Save As:** Use this option or choose File⇨Save when saving for the first time to open the Save/Save As dialog box (see Figure 1-15).

   - **Save as Web Page:** Use this command to save the design you create in PowerPoint as a Web page.

3. Name your file by typing a name in the File Name text box and locate a folder where you want to save the file.

4. Click Save to save the file.

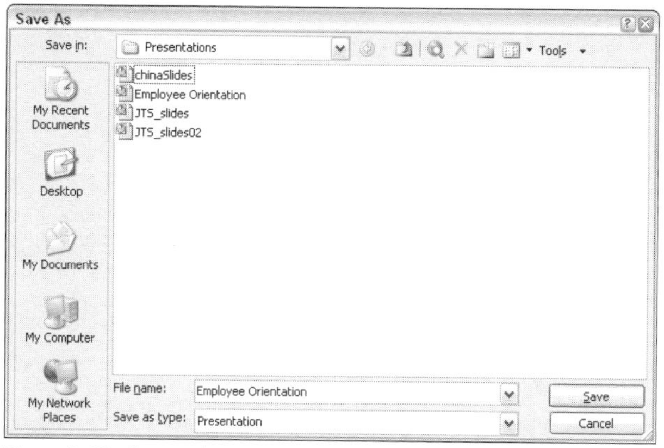

Figure 1-15: Choose File⇨Save As to save a PowerPoint presentation

Exit PowerPoint

1. Click the Close box in an open presentation document.

2. If you haven't saved the file since your last edit, PowerPoint prompts you with a dialog box to save your changes before the file closes (see Figure 1-16).

3. Click Yes to save your last edits. Click No to exit PowerPoint if you want to quit without saving your changes.

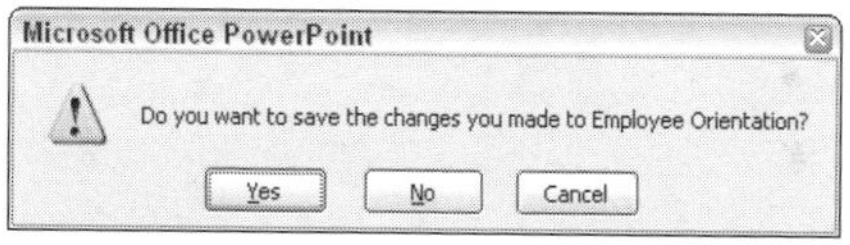

Figure 1-16: Click Yes to save your last edits before exiting PowerPoint or No to ignore edits made since the last save

Alternately, you can press Alt+F4 to exit PowerPoint.

Customizing the PowerPoint Interface

PowerPoint offers you much flexibility in customizing your work environment to suit your own personal editing needs. You can organize toolbars, open frequently used toolbars, add commands to toolbars, and work with expanded or shortened menus. All these options are available for you to create a work environment that accommodates your slide creation needs.

In addition to customizing the PowerPoint interface, we tossed in a little information on accessing help documents. After you get a handle on creating a blank presentation — the stuff we discuss in Chapter 1 — things can get a little complicated. Fortunately, PowerPoint offers you help every step along the way as you create your presentations.

Chapter

2

Get ready to . . .

Customize PowerPoint Tools

1. Open PowerPoint and choose Tools⇨Customize.

2. Click the Toolbars tab in the Customize dialog box (see Figure 2-1).

3. Check the boxes for all toolbars you want to display in PowerPoint.

 Depending on your editing tasks, you'll want to frequently visit the Customize dialog box to show toolbars according to the kind of edits you make on a slide presentation. For example, when working with tables, you'll want to display the Tables and Borders toolbar. Check the boxes for all tools pertaining to edits you make and turn them off by removing check marks when you no longer need a given toolbar.

4. Click Close and the toolbars you selected appear in the PowerPoint Document window.

Show Full Menus

1. Open PowerPoint and choose Tools⇨Customize.

2. Click the Options tab in the Customize dialog box (see Figure 2-2).

3. Check the Always Show Full Menus check box on the Options tab.

 By default, PowerPoint displays partial menus when you click a menu on the menu bar. When you pause a moment, the menu expands to a full menu where all the commands appear. As a matter of practice, you'll want to see all the menu commands during an editing session.

4. Click Close, and each time you open a menu, the full menu opens.

Figure 2-1: Click Toolbars and check the boxes for all toolbars you want to show in PowerPoint for a given editing session

Figure 2-2: Click Options and check the box for Always Show Full menus

Add a Command to a Toolbar

1. Open PowerPoint and choose Tools⇨Customize.

2. Click the Toolbars tab in the Customize dialog box.

3. Check a toolbar in the Toolbars list you want to customize.

4. Click the Commands tab.

5. Click a category in the left scrollable window.

6. Select a command from the right scrollable window.

7. Drag the command to the toolbar. In Figure 2-3, we added the Save As command to the Tables and Borders toolbar.

8. Click Close to dismiss the Customize dialog box.

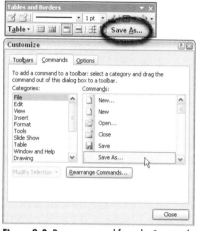

Figure 2-3: Drag a command from the Commands tab to a toolbar

Remove a Command from a Toolbar

1. Open PowerPoint, and choose Tools⇨Customize to open the Customize dialog box.

 When you remove a command from a toolbar, the Customize dialog box needs to be open.

2. Right-click the mouse button on the command you want to remove from the toolbar. Note that the Customize dialog box is open and you right-click the command in the toolbar.

3. Select Delete from the context menu (see Figure 2-4).

4. Click Close to dismiss the Customize dialog box.

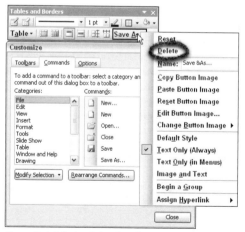

Figure 2-4: Selecting Delete from the context menu

Dock a Toolbar

1. Open PowerPoint and choose Tools⇨Customize.

2. Click the Toolbars tab in the Customize dialog box.

3. Check toolbars you want to display. Click OK and the toolbars appear in the Document window (see Figure 2-5).

 When you dock a toolbar, the toolbar is added in a row at the top of the PowerPoint window and remains stationary until you drag it to another location or close the toolbar.

4. Click and drag the toolbar up to the toolbar area in the PowerPoint window. As you approach the Standard toolbar, the toolbar snaps in position below the Standard toolbar.

5. Release the mouse button when the toolbar is in position.

 You can arrange toolbars in docked positions by dragging the separator bar appearing on the left side of each toolbar. Drag left and right to position horizontally or up and down to change the toolbar location.

6. Click and drag another toolbar to move it to position (see Figure 2-6).

 To undock a toolbar, click and drag the separator bar on the left side of the toolbar and away from the toolbar area. When a toolbar is floating again in the Document window, click the X appearing in the top-right corner of the toolbar to close it.

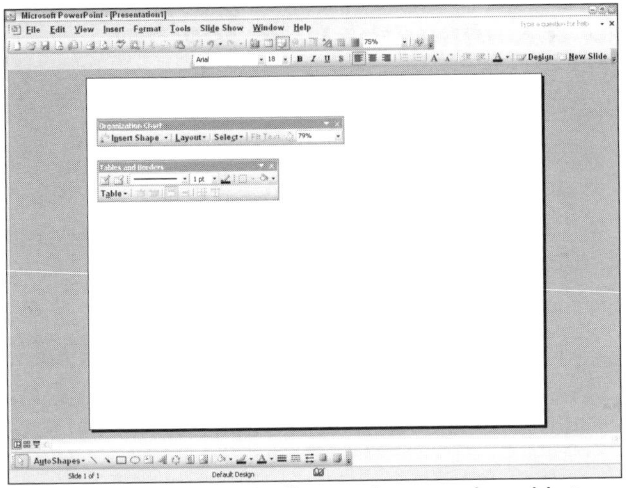

Figure 2-5: Toolbars are opened as floating toolbars scattered around the Document window

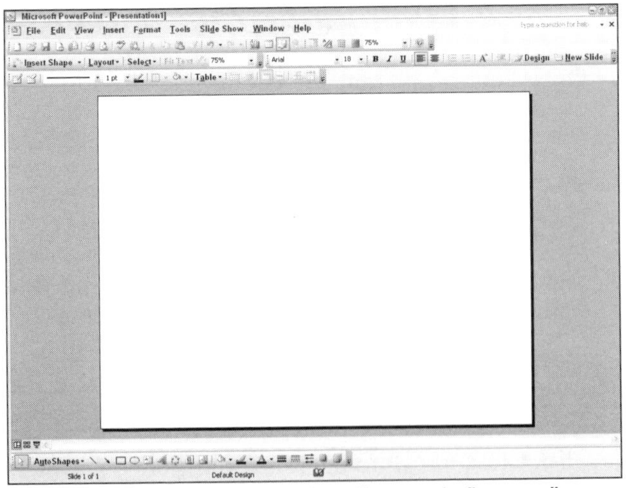

Figure 2-6: After dragging toolbars to the toolbar area, the floating toolbars are docked in position

Get Help in PowerPoint

1. Open PowerPoint and choose Help⇨Microsoft Office PowerPoint Help or press the F1 key on your keyboard. The PowerPoint Help pane opens on the right side of the PowerPoint window (see Figure 2-7).

    When accessing help information, you do not need to have a slide document open in PowerPoint.

2. To find help information, do one of the following:

   • Type a help topic to search in the Search For text box.

   • Click Table of Contents to browse the contents in the help document.

    If you want hard copy of a help item, you can easily print the help topic window by clicking on the Printer icon or pressing Ctrl+P. The Print dialog box opens. Make a selection for your printer and choose the page range for the pages to be printed.

3. Click a Table of Contents item to expand the topic. When you click a topic, subtopics and/or items display below a topic category.

4. Click an item in the contents list and the Help document displays information on the selected item.

5. To expand the pane so you can read more comfortably, place the cursor along the left edge of the Help document and drag left (see Figure 2-8).

6. To find help on additional topics, click the Table of Contents; the Help document changes to display information on the respective topic.

    The Microsoft Office PowerPoint Help document is an independent file. Move the document around by dragging the title bar. Minimize, maximize, and close the Help window by clicking the appropriate button in the top-right corner.

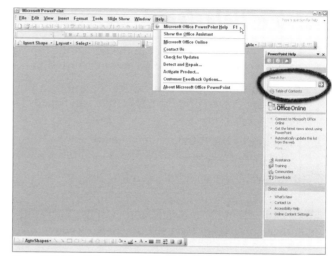

Figure 2-7: Select Help⇨Microsoft Office PowerPoint Help or press F1 to open the Help pane

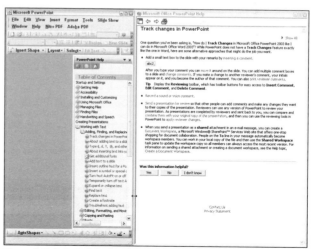

Figure 2-8: Drag the left edge of the Help pane to the left to open the pane to more easily read the help information

Search a Help Topic

1. Open PowerPoint and click in the box in the top-right corner where you see Type a Question for Help.

2. Type in a topic you wish to search for and then press Enter. The PowerPoint Search Results pane opens (see Figure 2-9).

3. Click one of the listed results. The Microsoft Office PowerPoint Help document opens in another window.

4. If you want to expand the window, drag the left edge to the left.

5. Click the X in the top-right corner of the Microsoft Office PowerPoint Help document to close the file.

Figure 2-9: Click a Search Result topic to open the Microsoft Office PowerPoint Help document

Use the Research Pane

1. With PowerPoint open, choose View⇨Task Pane.

2. Click Getting Started (or the item you see appearing at the top of the Task pane if another pane is open).

3. Select Research from the menu. The Research pane opens (see Figure 2-10).

4. Type an item to search in the Search For text box.

5. Select a research location from the drop-down menu below the Search For text box.

6. Press Enter on your keyboard to search the topic.

 The search locations offer many choices. You can select from a variety of reference books, research sites on the Web, and translate words among several languages. For more options with language translations, click the Translation Options link in the Translation pane. For more research options, click Research Options.

Figure 2-10: Type a topic or word to search and select a search location from the drop-down menu

Building Your Presentation and Adding Content

An outliner, among other things, makes PowerPoint the ideal presentation program. By importing text from a Microsoft Word document or typing text directly in PowerPoint in outline form, you can quickly apply text to slides when preparing a presentation. You can select a design template, type an outline, and finish your presentation within record time. When modifying a presentation is necessary, PowerPoint provides you options for rearranging slides, text on slides, and slide designs without spending time creating new documents.

In this chapter, you find out how to use PowerPoint's outliner feature, assemble some quick and easy presentations, and modify your presentation designs.

Chapter

3

Get ready to . . .

Create an Outline

1. Launch PowerPoint and create a new blank presentation.

 By default, a blank presentation opens when you launch PowerPoint. If you don't have a new blank slide in view in the PowerPoint Slides pane, choose File➪New or click the New button on the Standard toolbar.

2. Click the Outline tab to show the Outline pane (see Figure 3-1). Note that if the Outline tab is not Visible, choose View➪Normal.

3. Click the X in the Task pane to close the pane.

 You can leave the Task pane open while creating an outline; however, collapsing the pane provides you more viewing area on the slides. You can quickly bring the Task Pane back by pressing Ctrl+F1.

4. Click to the right of the small slide icon, type the main title in the title slide, and then do one of the following:

   - **Advance to the next slide:** If you want just a title to appear on the first slide, press Enter, and PowerPoint creates a second slide.

   - **Add a subtitle:** Press Ctrl+Enter and you stay on the same slide. Type a subtitle and then press Enter. Note that if you want to add a second subtitle to the same slide, just press Enter.

5. Type a slide title on slide 2 in the Outline tab and press Ctrl+Enter to add a bullet point. Press Ctrl+Enter to add additional bullet points.

6. Press Enter to create a new slide and repeat Step 5 to continue adding slides (see Figure 3-2).

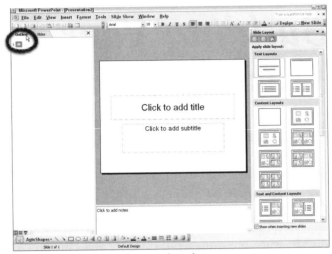

Figure 3-1: Click the Outline tab to open the Outline pane

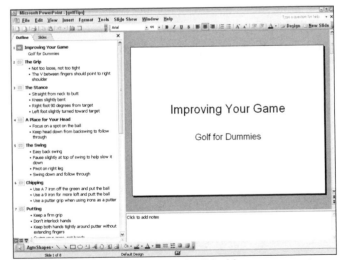

Figure 3-2: Add slide titles and bullet points for all the slides in your presentation

Import a Microsoft Word Document

1. Create a new blank presentation in PowerPoint.

2. Choose Insert⇨Slides from Files. The Slide Finder dialog box opens.

    If you have an outline created in Microsoft Word and formatted as an outline, choose Insert⇨Slides from Outline. PowerPoint imports the Word outline.

3. Click the Browse button in the Slide Finder dialog box to open the Browse dialog box (see Figure 3-3).

4. Select All Files from the Files of Type drop-down menu.

5. Click the Word document you want to import.

6. Click Open and you return to the Slide Finder dialog box (see Figure 3-4).

7. Click the right arrow at the bottom of the Slide Finder dialog box to scroll all the slides for a quick preview.

8. To import the Word text, do one of the following:

   • Click the Insert All button to insert all the Word text and create the slides as shown in the preview.

   • Click individual slides corresponding to the Word text you want to import. Then click the Insert button.

    The Slide Finder dialog box provides you with an option to see the Word text as either slides or as a list of slide titles. The default is the Slide view (as shown in Figure 3-4). Click the Title View icon to the far left of the Slide Finder dialog box, and the view changes to a list of slides by title.

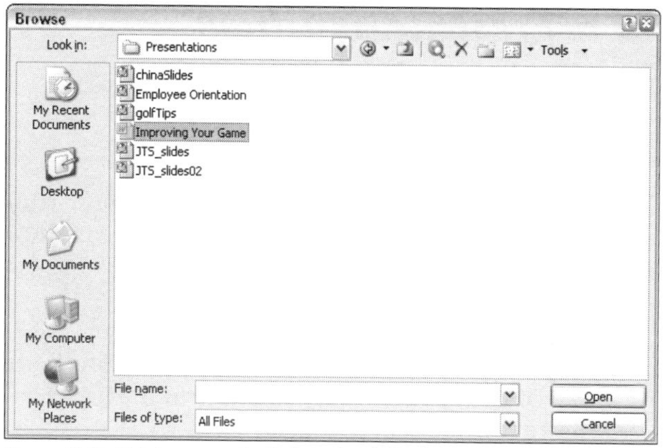

Figure 3-3: Click Browse in the Slide Finder dialog box to open the Browse dialog box

Figure 3-4: Choose the Word text you want to use

Send a Presentation from PowerPoint to Word

1. Create a slide presentation in PowerPoint.

2. Choose File➪Send To➪Microsoft Office Word. The Send to Microsoft Office Word dialog box opens, as shown in Figure 3-5.

3. Choose your page layout method:

   - **Notes Next to Slides:** The notes appear on the right side of each slide, with two slides to a page (see Figure 3-6).

   - **Blank Lines Next to Slides:** Blank lines appear on the right side of each slide.

   - **Notes Below Slides:** A page includes one slide with notes below each slide.

   - **Blank Lines Below Slides:** A Word page has one slide with blank lines below each slide.

   - **Outline Only:** Export just the text shown on the PowerPoint Outline tab to a Word file.

   - **Paste:** Paste the PowerPoint data in an existing Word document.

   - **Paste Link:** Link the PowerPoint data to an existing Word file.

4. Click OK. The file opens directly in Microsoft Word.

5. To save the Word file, choose File➪Save. Type a filename for the document, select a target folder, and click Save.

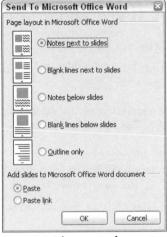

Figure 3-5: Select an option for exporting the PowerPoint file to a Word document

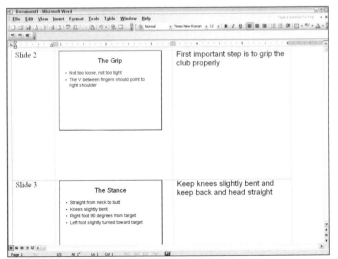

Figure 3-6: Here, your notes appear next to your slides

Change a Slide Master to a Title Master

1. Import a Microsoft Office Word document from either an outline or text document into PowerPoint by choosing Insert⇨Slides from Files.

     When you import a Word file in PowerPoint, all the text imports on slides are defined as slide masters. Most often, presentations contain one or more different slide masters, and the first slide is typically assigned to a title master slide. The title master design is your opening slide and may contain a title and subtitle.

2. Choose View⇨Task Pane to open the Task pane — if it is not already open. (See Chapter 1 for more information on using the Task Pane.)

3. Select Slide Layout from the Task pane's drop-down menu (see Figure 3-7). The Slide Layout pane includes different options available for different slide layouts. The top text layouts area in the pane contains four different layouts.

4. Click the first slide in the Slides pane and choose one of the following in the Text Layouts pane:

    -   **Title Slide:** Create the title slide design (see Figure 3-8).

    -   **Title Only:** Select this option if you don't have a subtitle on your opening slide.

    -   **Title and Text:** Leave this default as is if you want slides with titles and single-column bullet lists.

    -   **Title and 2-Column Text:** Select all slides but the first slide and click this option if you want to change the slides to a title and two-column text.

5. Choose File⇨Save and save your presentation.

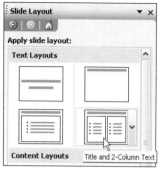

Figure 3-7: Select Slide Layout in the Task pane to open the Slide Layout pane

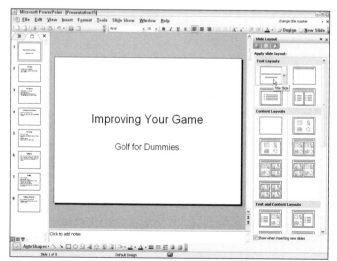

Figure 3-8: Click the first slide in the slide pane and click Title Slide

Apply a Slide Template

1. Create a new presentation or import a Word document in PowerPoint.

2. Define title and master slides by using the Slide Layout pane. (See Chapter 6 for more on defining title and master slides.)

3. Select Slide Design from the Task pane's drop-down menu.

4. Drag the slider bar on the right side of the Slide Design pane to scroll through the designs in the Apply a Design Template area.

5. Click the design you want in the Apply a Design Template area to apply the template to your presentation (see Figure 3-9).

6. Choose File➪Save to save your presentation.

Insert a New Slide

1. Open a presentation in PowerPoint.

2. Click the Slides tab to display the slides as thumbnails.

3. Click the slide preceding the slide you want to add in your presentation.

4. Choose Insert➪New Slide, press Ctrl+M (see Figure 3-10), or right-click and select New Slide.

5. Type text in either Slide mode or Outline mode for the title and bullet points.

6. Choose File➪Save or press Ctrl+S to save your edits.

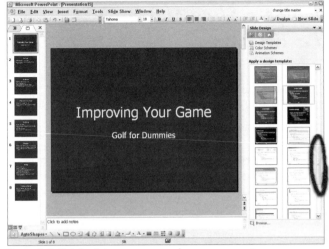

Figure 3-9: Click the design you want to apply to your presentation

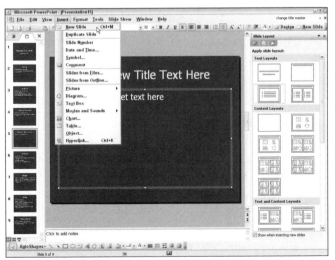

Figure 3-10: Here you can either choose Insert➪New Slide or press Ctrl+M

Insert a Slide from Another Presentation

1. Open a presentation in PowerPoint.

2. Click the Slides tab to show the slide thumbnails.

3. Choose Insert⇨Slides from Files. The Slide Finder dialog box opens.

4. Click the Browse button in the Slide Finder dialog box.

5. Navigate to the folder containing a presentation you want to use to import slides.

6. Select the presentation and click Open (see Figure 3-11).

7. While the Slide Finder dialog box remains open, click a slide in the Slides pane immediately preceding the place where you want the imported slides to appear.

 While the Slide Finder is open, you can click slides or outline topics without leaving the dialog box. All slides you import are inserted after the selected slide or outline topic.

8. After clicking Open, you return to the Slide Finder dialog box (see Figure 3-12). In the Slide Finder, do one of the following:

   • Click a slide in the Select Slides area of the Slide Finder. Then click the Insert button.

   • Press Ctrl and click the slides you want to import. Then click the Insert button.

   • Click Insert All to insert all slides in the open presentation.

9. Choose File⇨Save or press Ctrl+S to save your edits.

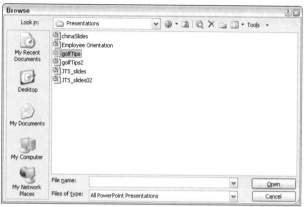

Figure 3-11: Click a presentation and click Open to import slides from one presentation to another

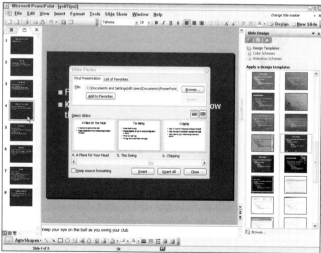

Figure 3-12: Click a slide in the Slide pane and click either Insert or Insert All to import slides

Display Multiple Presentations

1. Choose File➪Open and open a presentation in PowerPoint.

2. Repeat Step 1 until you've opened the files you need.

3. Choose Window➪Arrange All (see Figure 3-13).

Copy a Slide from Another Presentation

1. Open two slide presentations in PowerPoint.

2. Choose Window➪Arrange All.

 If you want the slides arranged with a particular file appearing on the left side of the PowerPoint window, select the presentation to make it the active window. When you choose Window➪Arrange All, the active presentation appears on the left side of the PowerPoint window.

3. Choose View➪Normal and click the Slides tab.

4. Click a slide in the presentation you want to copy and drag the slide thumbnail to the target file Slides tab where you want the copied slide to appear (see Figure 3-14).

 If you want to duplicate a slide in the same presentation, click a slide thumbnail and choose Edit➪Duplicate.

As you drag the thumbnail to the target Slides tab, notice that the cursor changes to an arrow with a plus symbol as it reaches the destination in the Outline/Slides tab. As you move the selection arrow to the target Slides tab, a horizontal bar indicates the insertion point.

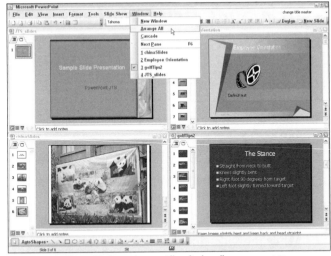

Figure 3-13: Choose Window➪Arrange All to display all open presentations

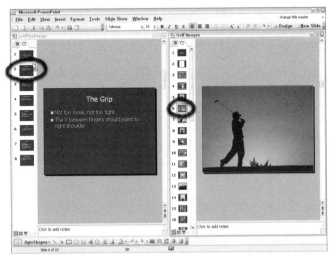

Figure 3-14: Copy a slide from the source file and paste it into the destination file
Photo courtesy PhotoDisc, Inc.

Paste a Slide from the Clipboard

1. Open a presentation containing a slide you want to copy.

2. Right-click a slide thumbnail in the Slides pane or some content on a slide.

    If you want to copy a slide with all the slide text, right-click a slide thumbnail in the Slides tab. If you want to copy some content, such as a picture or clip art, right-click an object on a slide.

3. Select Copy from the context menu (see Figure 3-15). Alternately, you can choose Edit⟹Copy or press Ctrl+C.

    Before you can paste Clipboard data, you must first copy data to the Clipboard. Any Copy command you use copies the selected slide or object to the Clipboard.

4. If you want to copy several items in one presentation and paste them in another presentation, click slides or objects and copy additional items to the Clipboard.

    As you copy additional items, the copied data is added to the Clipboard. Each item you copy in a PowerPoint session is accessible for pasting in another presentation.

5. Close the presentation after copying the data.

6. Choose File⟹Open and open a presentation where you want to paste the Clipboard data.

7. Choose View⟹Task Pane.

8. From the Task pane drop-down menu, select Clipboard.

9. Click a slide preceding the new slide you want to create.

10. Click the item in the Clipboard pane you want to paste as a new slide (see Figure 3-16).

Figure 3-15: Open a context menu and select Copy
Photo courtesy PhotoDisc, Inc.

Figure 3-16: Use the Clipboard to add content

Create a Default Slide Design

1. Open PowerPoint and create a new blank presentation.

2. Choose View⇔Task Pane to open the Task pane.

3. Select Slide Design from the Task pane drop-down menu.

4. Scroll through the designs in the Slide Design pane and select the slide design you want to use for a default.

5. Right-click the desired design and select Use for All New Presentations from the context menu (see Figure 3-17).

 After changing the default design, all new blank presentations you create in PowerPoint use the default design template. At any time, you can click another design to change the appearance of a presentation.

Edit a Slide Color Scheme

1. Open a presentation in PowerPoint.

2. Choose View⇔Task Pane to open the Task pane.

3. From the Task pane drop-down menu, select Slide Design–Color Schemes.

4. Click the color scheme you want to use in the Apply a Color Scheme area in the Slide Design pane (see Figure 3-18).

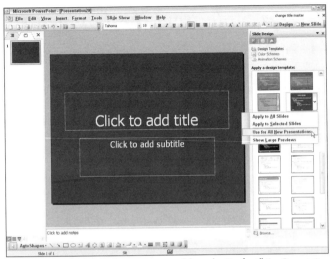

Figure 3-17: Right-click the design you want and then select Use for All New Presentations

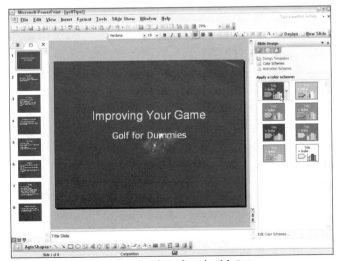

Figure 3-18: Click the desired color scheme from the Slide Design pane

Change Selected Slides' Color Schemes

1. Open a presentation in PowerPoint.

2. Choose View⟹Task Pane.

3. Select Slide Design–Color Schemes from the Task pane drop-down menu.

4. Open the Slides tab (if not already open) by choosing View⟹Normal and click Slides in the left pane.

5. Ctrl-click slides you want to change the current color scheme of while leaving the remaining slides deselected.

6. Right-click the new color scheme you want to use and select Apply to Selected Slides (see Figure 3-19).

 Normally you shouldn't change slides to different color schemes randomly in a presentation for good design practice. However, when you create custom design templates, you may want to use slight variations of color to identify different slide topics.

Show Large Design Previews

1. Open a presentation in PowerPoint.

2. Choose View⟹Task Pane.

3. Select Slide Design from the Task pane drop-down menu.

4. Right-click any design template in the Apply a Design Template area in the Task pane and select Show Large Previews from the context menu (see Figure 3-20).

 Showing large previews can help you see a design more clearly. When you first start using PowerPoint, you may want to keep the previews at larger sizes until you're more familiar with the layouts.

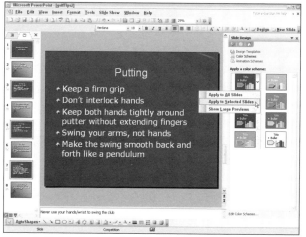

Figure 3-19: Selecting the Apply to Selected Slides command from the context menu

Figure 3-20: Right-click a design template and select Show Large Previews

Basic Editing Techniques

PowerPoint provides you with a number of editing features you can use to add some polish to your presentations. Using a design template starts you off with a particular preset format and layout. When you want to change design and layout, PowerPoint offers you the flexibility to modify text styles, bullet points, tabs and spacing, graphics, and just about any appearance you see on the slides.

In this chapter, you find out how to modify slides by using many PowerPoint commands and tools to customize presentations for your personal taste.

Chapter 4

Get ready to . . .

Edit Text on a Slide

1. Open a presentation in PowerPoint.

2. Choose View⇨Normal to open the Tabs pane or click the Normal View (Restore Panes) button in the lower-left corner of the PowerPoint window.

3. Click the Slides tab to view thumbnail images of the slides in your presentation (see Figure 4-1).

4. Click a slide thumbnail in the Slides tab to display the slide in the Slides pane.

5. Click the cursor inside the text placeholder below the title text placeholder on a slide.

6. Highlight the text you want to edit.

7. Type new text to replace the selected text.

Move Text on a Slide

1. With a presentation open in PowerPoint, click a slide in the Slides tab to place a slide in the Slides pane.

2. Click the cursor inside a text placeholder.

3. Move the cursor to the placeholder border so that it changes from an I-beam to a double-crossed arrow and then click the border (see Figure 4-2).

4. Drag the placeholder to a new position.

 Note that when you move a text placeholder, the placeholder moves only on the slide in view. All other text placeholders remain in the positions established on the master slide.

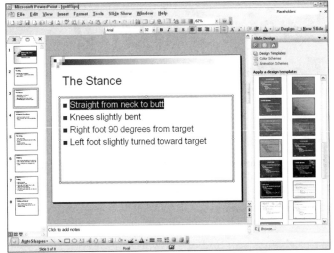

Figure 4-1: Click the Slides tab to view thumbnail images of the slides

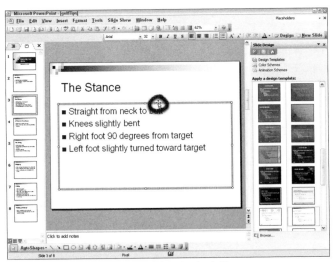

Figure 4-2: You can click a border and drag the placeholder to a new position

Move Text on a Master Slide

1. Open a presentation in PowerPoint.

2. Choose View⇨Master⇨Slide Master.

3. Click the text placeholder to select it.

4. Click the border and drag to a new position (see Figure 4-3).

5. Click Close Master View on the Slide Master View toolbar to return to the Normal slides view.

6. Press the Page Down key and view the slides in your presentation.

 All edits you make on the master slide apply to all the slides associated with that master.

Resize Text Boxes

1. Open a presentation in PowerPoint.

2. Choose View⇨Master⇨Slide Master.

 If you want to resize a text box on a single slide, select the slide on either the Outline or Slides tab to display the slide in the Slides pane.

3. Click either the title or the text placeholder depending on what placeholder you want to resize.

4. Drag any one of the small circles on the placeholder border in or out to size smaller or larger, respectively (see Figure 4-4).

5. Click Close Master View on the Slide Master View toolbar to return to Normal view.

Figure 4-3: Click and drag the placeholder to a new position on the master slide

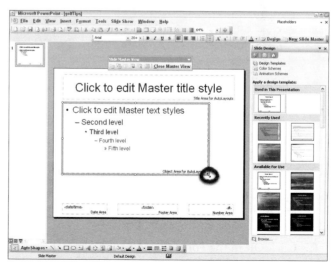

Figure 4-4: Click one of the circles and drag to resize the placeholder

Format Text Attributes

1. Open a presentation in PowerPoint.

2. Choose View➪Master➪Slide Master.

 If you want to change text attributes on a single slide, select the slide on either the Outline or Slides tab to display the slide in the Slides pane.

3. Click either the title or the text placeholder depending on what placeholder you want to edit the font(s).

4. Right-click the mouse and select Fonts from the context menu (see Figure 4-5). The Font dialog box opens (see Figure 4-6).

5. Choose from the following:

   - **Font:** Select a font.

   - **Font Style:** Select a font style.

   - **Size:** Select a size from the list or type a size in the text box.

   - **Effects:** Select from the different Effects options by checking the check boxes.

   - **Color:** Select a color from the drop-down menu. Select More Colors in the drop-down menu to create a custom color.

   - **Default for New Objects:** Check this box to apply the change as a new default for additional text place-holders you create.

   - **Preview:** Click Preview to show the results before dis-missing the Fonts dialog box.

6. Click OK in the Fonts dialog box to apply the attribute changes to the selected text.

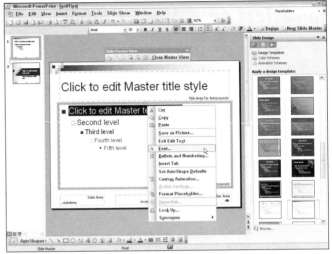

Figure 4-5: Select text and right-click the mouse to open a context menu

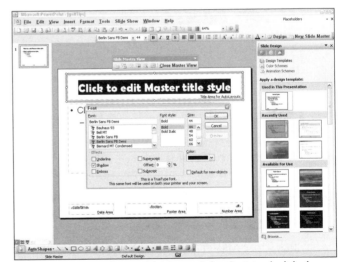

Figure 4-6: Set new attributes and click Preview before dismissing the dialog box

Adjust Line and Paragraph Spacing

1. Open a presentation in PowerPoint.

2. Choose View⇨Master⇨Slide Master.

 If you want to change line and paragraph spacing on a single slide, select the slide on either the Outline or Slides tab to display the slide on the Slides pane.

3. Click the text placeholder.

4. Right-click and select Format Placeholder from the context menu. The Format Auto Shape dialog box opens.

5. Click the Text Box tab (see Figure 4-7).

6. Select a text anchor point from the Text Anchor Point drop-down menu. The Text anchor point drop-down menu offers you options for anchoring text to the Top, Middle, Bottom, Top Centered, Middle Centered, and Bottom Centered position within the text placeholder rectangle.

7. Make changes for the internal margin as desired.

8. Click Preview before dismissing the dialog box.

9. Click OK.

10. Choose Format⇨Line Spacing to open the Line Spacing dialog box (see Figure 4-8).

11. Change line spacing options for Line Spacing, Before Paragraph, and/or After Paragraph as desired.

12. Click Preview to show the changes on the slide.

13. Click OK to accept the changes.

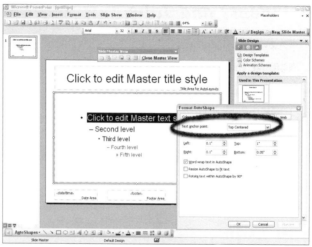

Figure 4-7: Click the Text Box tab to make changes to text alignment

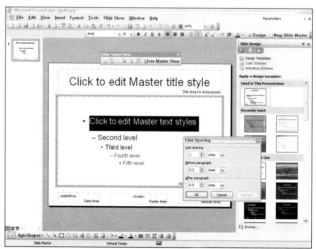

Figure 4-8: Adjust the line spacing and then click Preview to show the results

Set Indents and Tabs

1. Open a presentation in PowerPoint.

2. Choose View➪Master➪Slide Master.

3. Choose View➪Ruler (see Figure 4-9).

4. Click the text placeholder to select it.

5. Click the cursor in a line of text.

6. Click the tab selector on the left side of the ruler until the tab you want to use appears (see Figure 4-10). Your choices include the following:

   - **Indent Tabs.** The first two markers are used to set indents for leading indents and indentation.

   - **Left tab:** The first marker at 1.5 inches is the left tab marker. Left align text with this tab.

   - **Center tab:** The next marker is a center tab. Select this tab to center text.

   - **Right tab:** The next tab is the right tab. Right align text with this tab.

   - **Decimal tab:** Use the last marker to align decimal points.

7. Click the ruler where you want to add a tab. Click as many times as you want to place tabs at different ruler positions.

8. To move a tab, click it in the ruler and drag left or right.

9. To delete a tab, click the tab and drag below the ruler.

10. Click Close Master View to return to Normal view.

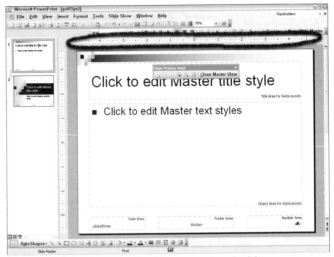

Figure 4-9: When Ruler is selected, a ruler appears above the slide

Figure 4-10: Click inside a body of text and the tabs appear on the horizontal ruler

Add a New Text Placeholder

1. Open a presentation in PowerPoint.

2. Choose View➪Master➪Slide Master.

3. Choose Insert➪Text Box.

4. The cursor changes shape to a cross. Click and drag a rectangle to shape the text box. Release the mouse button and the text box is shaped. A blinking cursor appears inside the box ready for you to type.

5. Type text in the box (see Figure 4-11).

6. Choose View➪Normal or click the Normal icon at the bottom of the Tabs pane.

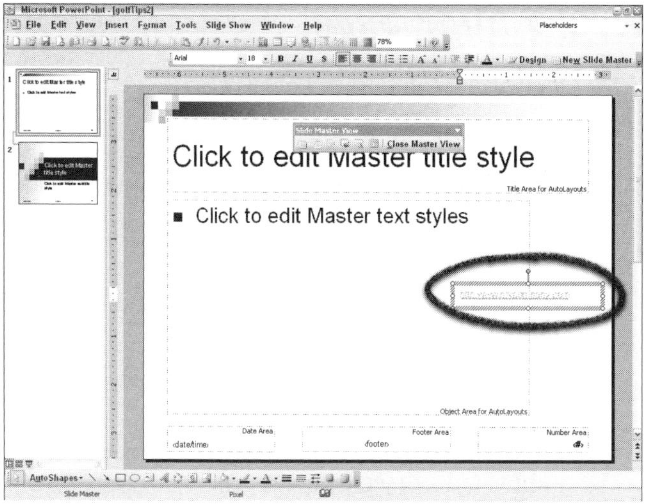

Rotate Text

1. Open a presentation in PowerPoint.

2. Choose View➪Master➪Slide Master.

3. Click a text placeholder to select it. The rotate handles appear.

4. Position the cursor over the rotate handle and the cursor changes to a semicircle with an arrowhead.

5. Rotate the text placeholder as you need (see Figure 4-12).

> You can rotate placeholders for text on either master slides or slides.

Figure 4-11: Add a text box and type text in the box

Figure 4-12: Position the cursor over the rotate handle

View a Slide Show

1. Open a presentation in PowerPoint.

2. Choose View⇨Slide Show or press F5.

 Alternatively, you can click the Slide Show from Current Slide button in the Status bar at the bottom of the Tabs pane (to the right of the Slide Sorter button).

3. Click buttons in the lower-left corner of the slide show window to do the following:

   • **Left arrow:** Navigate to the previous slide.

   • **Marker:** Open a pop-up menu where you can mark up a slide with comments or change selection arrow appearances (see Figure 4-13).

 For marking up text with highlights, select the Ballpoint Pen, the Felt Tip Pen, or the Highlighter and drag anywhere on a slide to make a highlight. Use the Eraser tools to eliminate markups. You can change markup colors by clicking Ink Colors and selecting a new color from a pop-up color palette.

   • **Navigation:** Open a pop-up menu where you can choose navigation and viewing options (see Figure 4-14).

   • **Right arrow:** Advance one slide.

4. Press the Esc key to exit Slide Show mode.

 If you add markups on slides, PowerPoint opens a dialog box after you press the Esc key to bail out of the Slide Show mode. To keep your markups, click Keep. To remove the markups, click Discard.

Figure 4-13: Click the highlighter icon and select an option from the pop-up menu

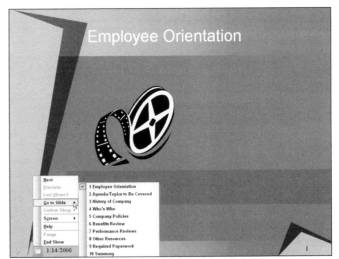

Figure 4-14: Open the Navigation pop-up menu to navigate slides

Organize Slides in the Slide Sorter

1. Open a presentation in PowerPoint.

2. Choose View➪Slide Sorter.

     Alternatively, you can click the Slide Sorter button in the Status bar below the Tabs pane. Note that the Slide Sorter button is to the right of the Normal View button.

3. Select a zoom level from the Zoom drop-down menu if the default is too small for you to read the slide content.

4. Click a slide thumbnail and drag it to a location between two slides.

5. As you drag a slide in the Slide Sorter, the cursor changes to display a dotted rectangle below the selection arrow. When you move a slide either between two slides or to the far left of a slide in a row, a vertical line appears, as shown in Figure 4-15. Release the mouse button and the slide drops between the slides on either side of the vertical line.

Delete a Slide

1. Open a presentation in PowerPoint.

2. Open the Slides tab.

3. Click a slide thumbnail of a slide you want to delete.

4. Right-click and select Delete Slide from the context menu (see Figure 4-16).

     Alternatively, you can press the Delete (Del) key on your keyboard or choose Edit➪Delete Slide.

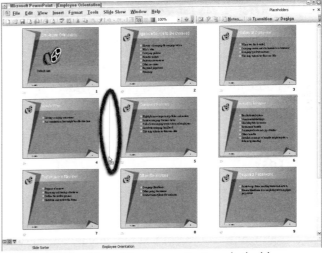

Figure 4-15: Click and drag a slide to a new position to reorder the slides

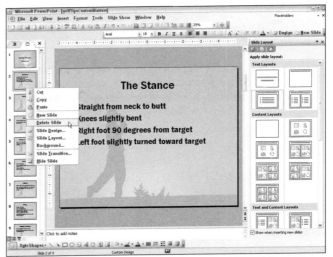

Figure 4-16: Select Delete Slide from the context menu to delete a slide

Copy and Paste between Slides

1. Open a presentation in PowerPoint.

2. Open the Slides tab and click a slide in your presentation.

3. Choose Insert⇨New Slide, press Ctrl+M, or right-click a slide in the Slides pane and select New Slide (Figure 4-17).

 Slides are inserted immediately after the slide in view in the Slides pane.

4. Click a slide in your presentation whose data you want to copy.

5. Highlight the object or text placeholder and choose Edit⇨Copy. You can also right-click and select Copy from the context menu or press Ctrl+C.

6. Click the new slide added to your presentation and choose Edit⇨Paste or right-click and select Paste from the context menu (see Figure 4-18).

 The item you paste is pasted at the same coordinates as where the item was copied from. If copying and pasting text placeholders, you can be certain the pasted placeholder appears at the same position as the one you copied.

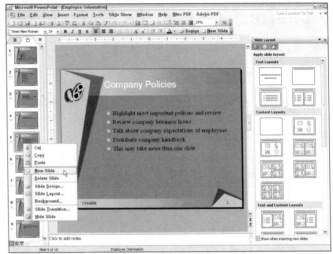

Figure 4-17: Insert a new slide where you want data pasted

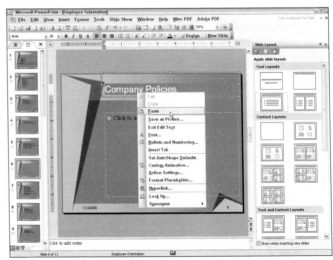

Figure 4-18: Right-click and select Paste from a context menu

Advanced Editing and Formatting

*I*n Chapter 4, we talk about some basic editing techniques for changing font attributes on title and master slides. More editing options are available to you for automating your workflow and checking your slides for spelling errors.

In this chapter, we talk about creating headers and footers, automating text formatting and corrections, and using PowerPoint's powerful spell checker.

Chapter

5

Get ready to . . .

Add Headers and Footers

1. Open a presentation in PowerPoint.

2. Open the Slides tab.

3. Click a slide to which you want to apply a header and/or footer.

 Ctrl+click to select multiple slides for adding a header and/or footer.

4. Choose View➪Header and Footer to open the Header and Footer dialog box (see Figure 5-1).

5. Make choices for the following:

   • **Date and Time:** Check the box and choose a date/time format from the drop-down menu.

 You can also insert a date and time by choosing Insert➪Date and Time. You get the same Header and Footer dialog box.

   • **Update Automatically:** Check the radio button to update the current date each time the presentation is opened.

   • **Fixed:** Click the Fixed radio button and type a date/time in the text box.

 When you include a date and time in your slide show, the date/time is derived from your system clock. When you add a fixed date/time, you can add any date/time value you desire in the text box.

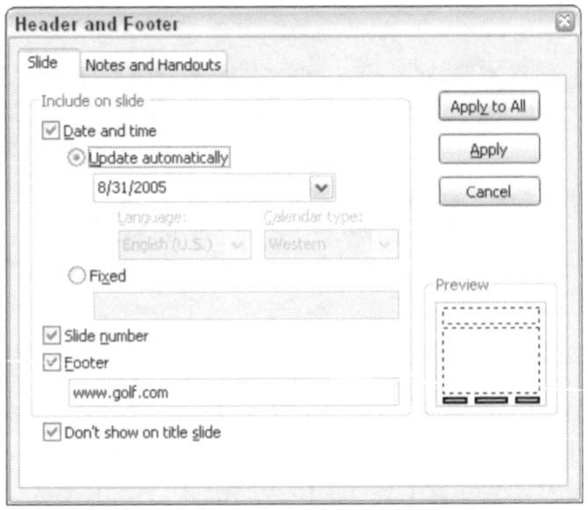

Figure 5-1: The Header and Footer dialog box

- **Slide Number:** Add a slide number to each slide.

- **Footer:** Add a footer. Type the footer text in the box.

- **Don't Show on Title Slide:** Check this box to keep the header/footer from appearing on the title slide.

- **Preview:** View the Preview area in the Header and Footer dialog box to see where the header/footer is placed on the slide. Note that when adding a footer as described here, three bold rectangles appear where the footer information is added.

6. Click Apply and the header/footer information is applied to the selected slides (see Figure 5-2). Click Apply to All to apply changes to all slides.

If you need to modify the placement of the header/footer information or the text attributes, choose View➪Master➪Slide Master. Select the text placeholders and right-click to open a context menu. Select Font to edit the font attributes. From the same context menu, select Format Placeholder to edit text alignment.

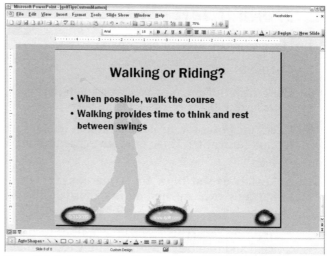

Figure 5-2: Settings made in the Header and Footer dialog box are applied to selected slides

Photo courtesy PhotoDisc, Inc.

AutoFormat Text

1. Open a presentation in PowerPoint.

2. Choose Tools⇨AutoCorrect Options.

3. Click the AutoFormat As You Type tab in the AutoCorrect dialog box (see Figure 5-3).

4. Check the boxes for the items you want to apply for autoformatting. Three categories appear in the dialog box:

   • **Replace as You Type.** Auto corrections for quotes, fractions, hyphens, and more are made while you type.

   • **Apply as You Type.** Formatting options such as bulleted and numbered lists and fitting text to frames is applied as you type.

   • **Apply as You Work.** As you work, automatic layout is applied to inserted objects.

    The AutoFit Title Text to Placeholder and AutoFit Body Text to Placeholder options make text fit within a text box or AutoShape. If you have too much text to fit within a placeholder, the text is automatically downsized so all text can fit within the placeholder.

5. Leave all the check boxes checked as set by the program default and click OK.

6. Open a slide to edit by clicking a slide thumbnail in the Slides tab.

7. Type **:-)** (colon, dash, right parenthesis). The AutoFormat uses a smiley face for the text as it was defined in the AutoFormat options (see Figure 5-4).

Figure 5-3: Check items to which you want to apply autoformatting

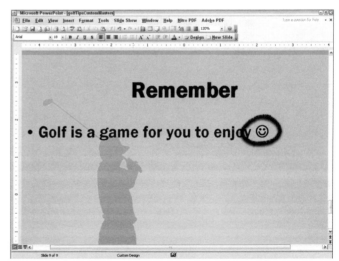

Figure 5-4: The Smiley Face autocorrect option changes the typed characters to a graphic

Use AutoCorrect

1. Open a presentation in PowerPoint.

2. Choose Tools⇨AutoCorrect Options.

3. Click the AutoCorrect tab to open the AutoCorrect: *(language)* dialog box.

 Note *(language)* is the default language installed with your PowerPoint application. If the installation was made for U.S. English, the title of the dialog box is AutoCorrect: English (U.S.).

4. Select options by checking the boxes for the items you want PowerPoint to autocorrect as you type (see Figure 5-5).

5. Type an item in the Replace text box and a replacement item in the With text box. For example, type **dollar** in the Replace text box and $ in the With text box. Each time you type **dollar**, the symbol $ is automatically substituted.

6. Click the Add button for each item you add for replacement.

7. Click Exceptions to open the AutoCorrect Exceptions dialog box (see Figure 5-6).

8. Type words you don't want PowerPoint to capitalize when typed as the first word in a sentence. For example, a word like *eMail*.

9. Click the INitial CAps tab.

10. Type words or acronyms in which you want multiple caps in a word — something like IQ.

11. Click OK in the AutoCorrect Exceptions dialog box.

12. Click OK in the AutoCorrect: *(language)* dialog box.

Figure 5-5: Select items you want PowerPoint to autocorrect

Figure 5-6: Click Exceptions to open the AutoCorrect Exceptions dialog box

 Choices you make in the AutoCorrect: *(language)* dialog box and the AutoCorrect Exceptions dialog box become new defaults and apply to all presentations you create and/or edit.

Spell Check Slides

1. Open a presentation in PowerPoint.

2. Choose Tools⇨Spelling or press F7 to open the Spelling dialog box (see Figure 5-7).

3. Click one of the following:

   - **Ignore/Ignore All:** Click Ignore to ignore a word you know is spelled correctly. Click Ignore All if the word is repeated in your presentation.

   - **Change/Change All:** Accept PowerPoint's suggestion in the Change To text box by clicking Change or Change All. If PowerPoint provides no suggestion, type the correct spelling in the Change To text box.

   - **Add:** Click Add if you want to add a word to a custom dictionary.

   - **Suggest:** Click Suggest, and PowerPoint provides one or more options in the Suggestions list.

   - **AutoCorrect:** Click AutoCorrect to add a word to the AutoCorrect list. When you type the word again on a slide, PowerPoint autocorrects any misspelling you might type for the word.

   - **Close:** Click Close when finished spell checking.

4. Click Close after performing a spell check.

5. Choose Tools⇨Options.

6. Click Spelling and Style in the Options dialog box (see Figure 5-8).

7. Select options on the Spelling and Style tab.

8. Click OK to exit the Options dialog box.

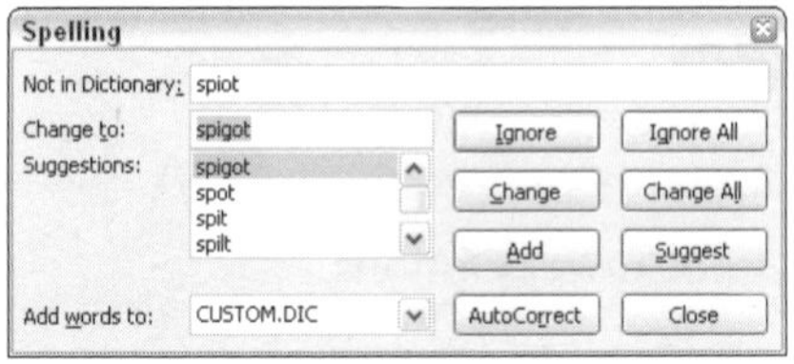

Figure 5-7: Choose Tools⇨Spelling to open the Spelling dialog box

Figure 5-8: Check options you want for spell checking and click OK

Find and Replace Words

1. Open a presentation in PowerPoint.

2. Choose Edit⇨Find or press Ctrl+F to open the Find dialog box (see Figure 5-9).

3. Type a word you want to find in your presentation in the Find What text box.

4. Check the following boxes to narrow your search:

   • **Match Case:** Check this box to match letter case.

   • **Find Whole Words Only:** Check this box to locate whole words and not word stems.

5. Click Find Next to find the next occurrence of the word.

6. Click Close to close the Find dialog box.

7. Choose Edit⇨Replace to open the Replace dialog box (see Figure 5-10).

8. Type a word to find in the Find What text box.

9. Type a word you want to use to replace the found word(s) in the Replace With text box.

10. Check the boxes for Match Case and Find Whole Words Only if they apply.

11. Do one of the following:

    • Click Replace to replace a single instance of the found word. You can click the Find Next button to locate another instance.

    • Click Replace All to replace all instances of a found word.

12. Click Close after replacing all the words you want to replace.

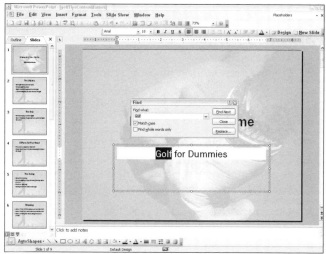

Figure 5-9: Type a word to find in the Find What text box
Photo courtesy PhotoDisc, Inc.

Figure 5-10: Click Close when finished replacing words

Copy Text Formatting Using Format Painter

1. Open a presentation in PowerPoint.

   If you want to copy formatting from one presentation to another, open a second presentation.

2. Choose View➪Normal to open the Tabs pane or click the Normal View (Restore Panes) button in the Status bar in the lower-left corner of the PowerPoint window.

3. Click the cursor in a text placeholder whose formatting you want to copy and apply to a different slide or different presentation.

4. Click the Format Painter tool on the Standard toolbar (see Figure 5-11).

5. Click a slide in the Slides pane to which you want to apply the same style.

6. When you click the Format Painter tool, the cursor changes to an I-beam with a paintbrush, as shown in Figure 5-12. Move the cursor to a text placeholder and drag across the text line to which you want to apply the copied style. The same text attributes (font, style, point size, color) from the text you originally clicked with the Format Painter tool are applied to the target slide.

   If you want to apply a style to several slides, double-click the Format Painter tool. Click and drag across text you want to change. Press the Page Down key to scroll slide pages and select more text to change. Repeat the steps to change all the text you want to change. When you finish, click the Format Painter tool again to turn it off or press the Esc key.

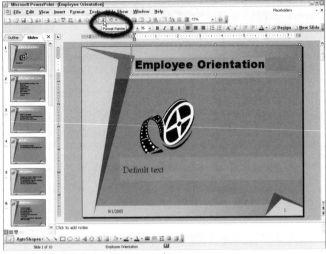

Figure 5-11: Click the Format Painter tool

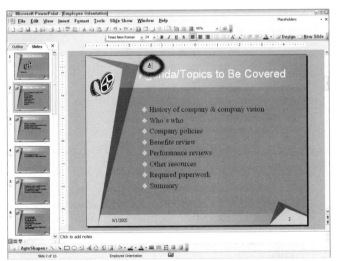

Figure 5-12: Click with the Format Painter tool in a text placeholder to apply the copied style to another slide

Working with Masters

Master slides provide you options for globally changing the design of your presentations. With a quick reorganization and formatting for text — or a change in the graphic images on a master slide — you can apply changes to all slides in your presentation in a matter of minutes.

PowerPoint provides you with four different master slides. The title master and slide master affect the design of your presentation. The note master and handout master handle the designs for notes and handouts.

In this chapter, you find out how to edit and change all master slides and apply the changes to your presentation.

Chapter

6

Get ready to . . .

Create a Title Master

1. Open a PowerPoint Presentation where you want to change the master slides.

2. Choose View⇨Master⇨Slide Master.

3. The Slide Master View toolbar opens(see Figure 6-1). Your options here are as follows:

    *   **Insert New Slide Master:** Create a new slide master.

    *   **Insert New Title Master:** Create a new title master slide.

    *   **Delete Master:** Delete the master slide currently in view.

    *   **Preserve Master:** Protect both the title master and slide master against additional changes. After clicking the tool, a pushpin icon appears adjacent to the left side of the slide thumbnails on the Slide Master tab. Click the tool again to unprotect the masters.

    *   **Rename Master:** Type a name for your master in the dialog box that opens.

    *   **Master Layout:** Each master title slide contains five placeholders. By default, all the placeholders appear on a new title slide when you create it. If you delete a placeholder and want to restore it, click this tool and the Master Layout dialog box opens. Check the box for the missing placeholder and it is restored.

    *   **Close Master View.** Click this button to dismiss the Slide Master View toolbar and exit master editing mode.

4. Click the Insert New Title Master button to create a new title master (see Figure 6-1).

5. Click the mouse cursor in the Title placeholder to select it.

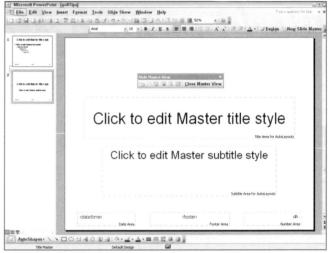

Figure 6-1: The Slide Master View toolbar

Figure 6-2: Select Font from the context menu to open the Font dialog box

6. Right-click the mouse button and select Font from the context menu. The Font dialog box opens (see Figure 6-2).

7. Scroll the Font window and select a new font, font style, and font size.

8. Click Preview to preview the text.

9. Click OK and click in the Text placeholder to select the text.

10. Right-click and select Font from the context menu.

11. Change font attributes for the selected text.

12. Choose Insert⇨Picture⇨From File to open the Insert Picture dialog box.

13. Select a picture to use as the background in the Insert Picture dialog box and click the Insert button.

Keep in mind that inserted pictures appear in the foreground, hiding the text on your slide. After inserting a picture, you need to move the picture behind the text.

14. Right-click the inserted picture and choose Order⇨Send to Back (see Figure 6-3).

15. Click Close Master View on the Slide Master View toolbar to dismiss the toolbar and return to Normal view.

16. Click the first slide in your presentation in the Slides pane.

17. Click Title Slide in the Slide Layout pane; the new title master is applied to your opening slide (see Figure 6-4).

You can also create a new presentation from scratch and add custom master slides. Open PowerPoint and click the New button on the Standard toolbar; then follow the remaining steps for creating a new Title slide.

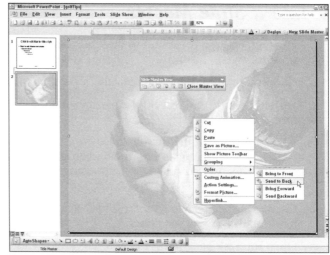

Figure 6-3: Order⇨Send to Back moves the picture behind the text
Photo courtesy PhotoDisc, Inc.

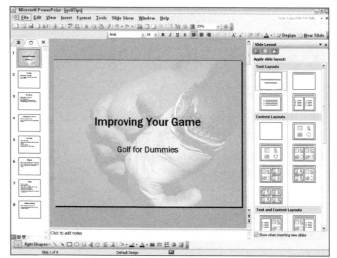

Figure 6-4: A new title slide is added to the presentation

Create a Slide Master

1. Open an existing presentation or create a new presentation in PowerPoint.

2. Choose View➪Master➪Slide Master (see Figure 6-5).

3. Format the title and text on the master slide for font, font style, and font size.

4. Insert a picture on the master slide if you like and be certain to send the picture to the background by right-clicking the inserted picture and choosing Order➪Send to Back.

5. Click Close Master View on the Slide Master View toolbar to return to Normal view.

6. Open the Task pane (Ctrl+F1) and select Slide Design from the drop-down menu. Your new slide master appears in the Apply a Design Template area in the Slide Design pane.

7. Open the Slides tab if it is not in view and click the second slide in the presentation.

8. Scroll the Slides tab to place the last slide thumbnail in view.

9. Press the Shift key and click the last slide thumbnail.

10. Right-click the new slide master design in the Slide Design pane (see Figure 6-6).

11. Click Apply to Selected Slides to apply the new master slide to all slides selected in the Slides tab.

Figure 6-5: Changing from Normal view to Master Editing view

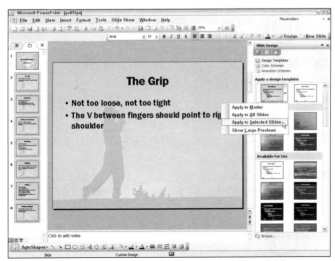

Figure 6-6: Select slides in the Slides tab and select Apply to Selected Slides
Photo courtesy PhotoDisc, Inc.

Create Multiple Slide Masters

1. Open an existing presentation in PowerPoint.

2. Choose View⇨Master⇨Slide Master.

3. Edit the current master slide for font attributes, adding a picture or changing background colors.

4. Click the Rename Master button on the Slide Master View toolbar and type a name for the master.

5. Click the Insert New Master Slide button on the Slide Master View toolbar to create a second master slide.

6. Edit the slide for font and background.

7. Click the Rename Master button and type a new master slide name in the Rename dialog box (see Figure 6-7).

8. Click Close Master View on the Slide Master View toolbar.

9. Press the Ctrl key and click each slide thumbnail in the Slides tab that you want to apply one master slide.

10. Open the Slide Design pane and click the slide master you want to apply to the selected slides.

11. Press Ctrl and click the remaining slides in the Slides tab that you want to apply your second master.

12. Click the second master slide in the Slide Design pane (see Figure 6-8).

 Note that a tool tip opens when the cursor appears over a master slide in the Slide Design pane and reports all slides, according to slide number, that use the slide appearing below the cursor.

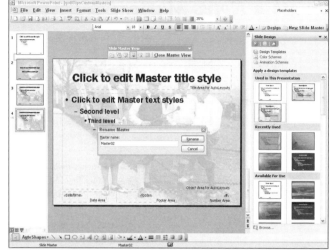

Figure 6-7: The Rename Master dialog box
Photo courtesy Corbis Digital Stock

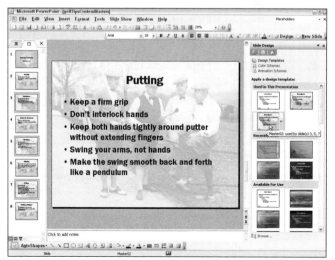

Figure 6-8: Applying different master slides to selected slides

Create a Notes Master

1. Open an existing presentation in PowerPoint.

2. Choose View⇨Master⇨Notes Master.

3. Right-click the Note Master and select Notes Background (see Figure 6-9).

4. Edit the color and fill effects by making selections in the Notes Background dialog box.

 If you want to add a graphic image to the Notes pages, select Insert⇨Picture. Select from the submenu either Clip Art (to add a clipart image) or From File (to add a graphic you created and saved as a file). When the object is inserted on the Notes master page, move the object below the slide. Objects placed on the slides themselves won't be visible on the notes pages.

5. Click Apply to change the background color and fill effect.

6. Click the Close Master View button on the Notes Master View toolbar to return to Normal view.

7. Choose View⇨Notes Page.

8. Click the cursor in the text box and type the notes you want to appear for the slide in view (see Figure 6-10).

9. Press the Page Down key on your keyboard to advance to the next slide.

10. Type text in the notes text box to add note text to the slide in view.

11. Continue advancing slides and adding note text for each slide.

12. Choose File⇨Save to update your presentation.

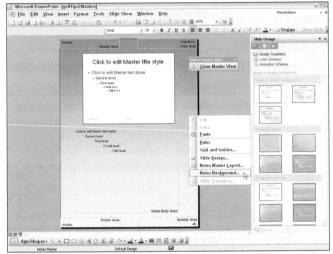

Figure 6-9: Select Notes Background

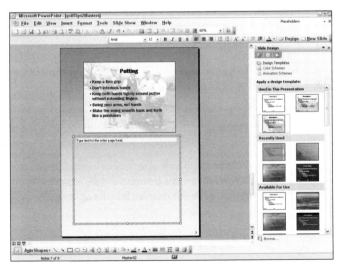

Figure 6-10: Click the cursor in the notes text box and type your note text

Create a Handout Master

1. Open an existing presentation in PowerPoint.

2. Choose View➪Handout Master.

3. Click a handout layout style on the Handout Master View toolbar (see Figure 6-11).

 As you click different layout options on the Handout Master View toolbar, the Handout Master reflects changes made to the design. You have options for handouts displaying one or several slides per page. The dotted lines represent the slide images and the blank space is designed for your presentation audience to add personal notes.

4. Click the Close Master View button on the Handout Master View toolbar to return to Normal view.

5. Choose File➪Print Preview.

6. Open the Print What drop-down menu and select an option from the menu choices for the number of slides you want to appear on each handout page (see Figure 6-12).

7. Preview the handout design.

8. Click Close in the Print Preview dialog box to return to Normal view.

9. Choose File➪Save to save your edits.

Figure 6-11: Click a layout style on the Handout Master View toolbar

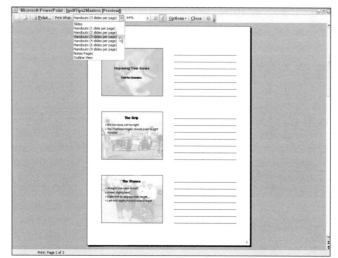

Figure 6-12: Selecting the number of slides to appear per printed page

Part II
Adding Visual Interest to Slides

The 5th Wave · By Rich Tennant

"What do you mean you need it for your class PowerPoint presentation?"

Adding Lines and Shapes

If a picture is what you want to communicate a message, then PowerPoint's drawing options are your ticket to creating graphic representations of ideas and concepts. Using drawing tools and autoshapes, you can create visual messages utilizing free form drawing tools and predefined shapes.

With the ease of drawing lines and geometric shapes or selecting graphic objects from a number of different palettes, you can quickly assemble a diagram or drawing to illustrate your point. In this chapter you learn how to use the many different tools in PowerPoint to create graphic objects and images.

Chapter
7

Get ready to . . .

Use the Drawing Toolbar

1. Create a new blank presentation in PowerPoint by clicking the New button on the Standard toolbar.

2. Click the text placeholders and press the Delete (Del) key on your keyboard.

3. Choose View➪Toolbars➪Drawing to open the Drawing toolbar (see Figure 7-1).

 The Drawing toolbar may be docked at the bottom of the PowerPoint window. To move the toolbar to the top level or move it to the Document window as a floating toolbar, click the separator bar on the far left side of the toolbar and drag to move it.

4. Choose from one of the following tools:

   - **Autoshapes:** You can select from a number of different shapes to add to your slide.

   - **Line:** Click the Line tool and drag the cursor in the Slide window to create a line.

   - **Arrow:** Draw a line with an arrowhead.

   - **Rectangle:** Draw a rectangle. To draw a square, press the Shift key.

   - **Oval:** Draw ovals and circles.

   - **Text Box:** Click the Text Box tool and drag with your mouse to create a text placeholder for the rectangle.

   - **Insert WordArt:** Open the WordArt Gallery to choose from a variety of stylized text.

   - **Insert Diagram or Organizational Chart:** Click one of the gallery items in the Diagram Gallery (see Figure 7-2) and then click OK to add that diagram to your slide page.

Figure 7-1: The Drawing toolbar

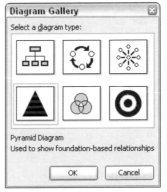

Figure 7-2: Click the Insert Diagram or Organizational Chart tool to open the Diagram Gallery

- **Insert Clip Art:** Select a clip art object from the Clip Art pane and drag it to the slide in view. Drag to position on the slide. (see Figure 7-3).

- **Insert Picture:** Select an image in the Insert Picture dialog box, then click the Insert button to import the image on your slide.

- **Fill Color:** Select a preset color from the drop-down menu or click More Fill Colors to open the Windows System color palette.

- **Line Color:** Select your linen then click the Line Color tool to open a drop-down menu where you can change a line's color.

- **Font Color:** Select your text, then click the Font Color tool and select a color to change the font color.

- **Line Style:** The Line Style drop-down menu provides options for changing the style of lines in terms of point size and multiple lines.

- **Dash Style:** The Dash Style drop-down menu lets you select from a different number of dashed line styles.

- **Arrow Style:** The Arrow Style drop-down menu lets you select an end point shape. To create custom line and arrowhead shapes, select More Arrows from the drop-down menu to open the Format Autoshape dialog box.

- **Shadow Style:** The Shadow Style drop-down menu lets you select from different drop shadow appearances. To customize the shadows for offset distances, select Shadow Settings to open the Shadow Settings toolbar.

- **3-D Style:** The 3-D Style drop-down menu lets you select 3-D styles for your 2-D objects. At the bottom of the menu, you can select 3-D Settings to open the 3-D Settings toolbar where you can make custom appearances on the selected object (see Figure 7-4).

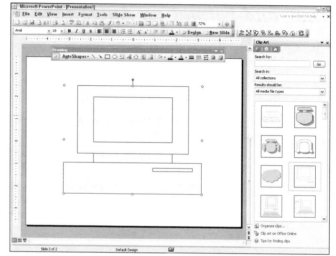

Figure 7-3: Click the Clip Art button to open the Clip Art pane

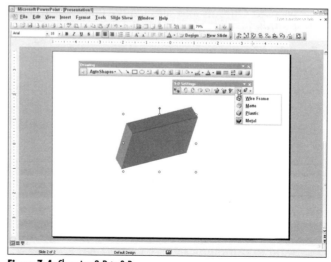

Figure 7-4: Changing 2-D to 3-D

Draw and Format an AutoShape

1. Create a blank presentation by clicking the New button on the Standard toolbar.

2. Choose View⇨Toolbars⇨Drawing to open the Drawing toolbar.

3. Click the Insert Clip Art button on the Drawing toolbar to open the Clip Art pane.

4. Click an object in the pane and drag it to the blank slide.

 If you want more clip art choices than you see in the Clip Art pane, click Clip Art on Office Online at the bottom of the Clip Art pane. Your Web browser takes you to the Microsoft Web site where you can obtain free clip art images.

5. Click the AutoShapes button on the Drawing toolbar.

6. Select a menu item and then an object. In this example, we used Callouts and selected the Rounded Rectangular Callout (see Figure 7-5).

7. Release the mouse button and the cursor changes to a crosshair.

8. Draw the shape you desire and then release the mouse button; the autoshape appears on the slide.

9. Use the Fill Color tool from the Drawing toolbar to fill it with color

10. Click the Text Box tool on the Drawing toolbar (or press F2 with an object selected) and start typing.

11. Click and drag a rectangle to define the size of a new text placeholder somewhere inside your autoshape.

12. Type text to add new text that describes the point you want to communicate (see Figure 7-6).

Figure 7-5: Select an item on one of the submenus

Figure 7-6: Add text to an autoshape to communicate an idea to your audience

Use WordArt to Jazz Up Text

1. Create a new blank slide.

2. Open the Drawing toolbar by choosing View⇨Toolbars⇨Drawing.

3. Click the WordArt button on the Drawing toolbar to open the WordArt Gallery (see Figure 7-7).

4. Click a style you want to use for new text on your slide and then click OK in the WordArt Gallery.

5. The Edit WordArt Text dialog box opens. In the dialog box, do the following:

- Select a font from the Font drop-down menu.

- Select a point size from the Size drop-down menu.

- Select B for Bold and I for Italic if you want either or both styles applied to your text.

- Type the text you want to appear on your slide in the Text window.

6. Click OK and the text drops on the slide.

 When the WordArt text appears on your slide and the text is selected, the WordArt toolbar opens. You can make further formatting changes to the text — such as fill colors and patterns — by clicking buttons on the toolbar.

7. Click a circle on the border and drag in or out to size the text.

8. To change the text color, click the Format WordArt button on the WordArt toolbar (see Figure 7-8). The Format WordArt dialog box opens where you can change the color and adjust the transparency settings.

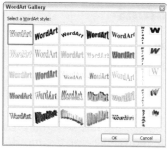

Figure 7-7: Select a style and click OK

Figure 7-8: Use the WordArt toolbar for any additional formatting

Draw and Group Lines

1. Create a new blank slide.

2. Open the Drawing toolbar by choosing View↝ Toolbars↝Drawing.

3. Click the Line button on the Drawing toolbar.

4. Click and drag a line. To keep the line straight, press the Shift key as you drag the mouse. Release the mouse button to complete drawing the line.

5. Draw a second line on the same slide.

6. Select both lines by clicking one line and Shift+clicking the second line.

7. Right-click and choose Grouping↝Group (see Figure 7-9).

 When you group lines together, you can easily change line attributes and size the lines together when they are grouped.

Change a Line Style

1. Create one or more lines on a slide.

2. If creating more that one line, be sure to group them.

3. Be certain the line (or group) is selected and then right-click and select Format AutoShape from the context menu. The Format AutoShape dialog box opens (see Figure 7-10).

4. Use the various drop-down menus in the Line area to format your selection as desired.

5. Click OK to change the line attributes.

Figure 7-9: Choose Grouping↝Group to group lines together

Figure 7-10: Change line attributes in the Format AutoShape dialog box

Add Arrowheads to Lines

1. Open the Drawing toolbar by choosing View⇨ Toolbars⇨Drawing.

2. Do one of the following:

   • Click the Arrow button on the Drawing toolbar and drag the mouse to create a line. The arrowhead appears at the end point.

   • Click the Line button on the Drawing toolbar and draw a line on your slide.

    If you want a default arrowhead to appear on a line, use the Arrow button. If you want to modify arrowheads, you can use either tool to create a line.

3. Right-click a line and select Format AutoShape to open the Format AutoShape dialog box — or just double click the line to open the same dialog box.

4. Select from the drop-down menus in the Arrows section for beginning and ending styles (see Figure 7-11), then click OK.

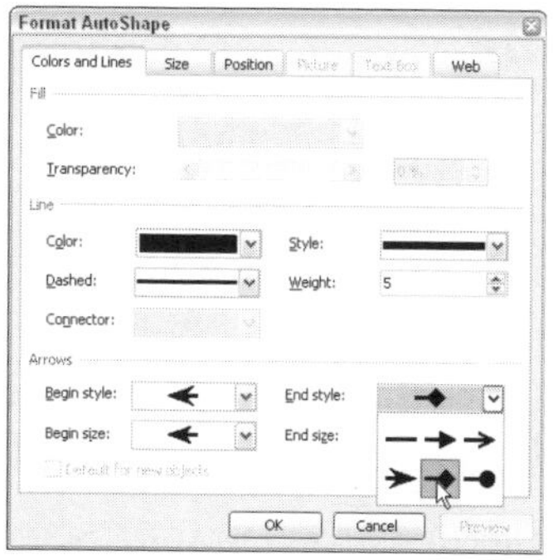

Create Block Arrows

1. Open the Drawing toolbar by choosing View⇨ Toolbars⇨Drawing.

2. Click the AutoShapes button to open the AutoShapes drop-down menu.

3. Select Block Arrows from the menu options.

4. Click a style for the arrow you want to add to your slide (see Figure 7-12).

5. Click and drag the mouse to create the shape at the desired size.

Figure 7-11: Format arrowheads in the Arrows section

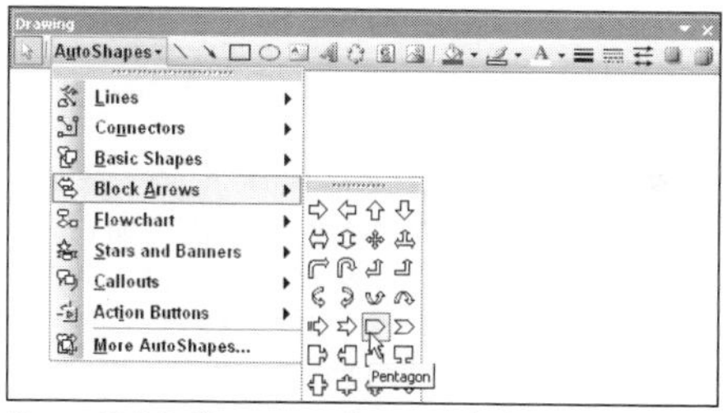

Figure 7-12: Choose AutoShapes⇨Block Arrows to select a block arrow style

 If you want to add some flair to the design of block arrows, click the 3-D Style button on the Drawing toolbar and select a 3-D style. Additionally, you can add a drop shadow by clicking the Shadow Style button and selecting a shadow type from the drop-down menu.

Draw a Curved Line

1. Open the Drawing toolbar by choosing View⇨ Toolbars⇨Drawing.

2. Select AutoShapes on the Drawing toolbar to open the drop-down menu.

3. Select Basic Shapes and click the Arc shape on the submenu (see Figure 7-13).

If you want to draw a freeform line instead of an arc shape, choose AutoShapes⇨Lines and click on the Curve line or the Scribble tool in the Lines submenu.

4. Click and drag the mouse to create the arc shape.

5. To reshape the line, click and drag the end points.

You can drag end points to size the line and reshape the path by dragging the line end points appearing as diamonds on either side of the line. Additionally, you can resize the shape by clicking the circles and dragging in or out to resize the entire shape. You can also rotate the shape by dragging the rotate handle.

6. After reshaping, click the line to select it.

7. Right-click and select Format AutoShape from the context menu — or just double click the line. The Format AutoShape dialog box appears (see Figure 7-14).

8. Select options from the drop-down menus in the Line area of the Colors and Lines tab.

9. Click Preview to preview the results.

10. Click OK when the shape appears as you like.

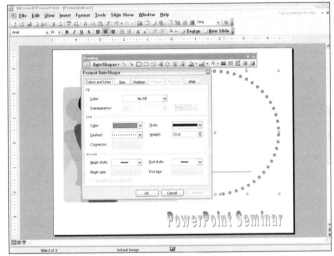

Figure 7-13: Select the Arc shape to draw a curved line

Figure 7-14: The Line area of the Colors and Lines tab

Move Lines and Shapes

1. Create a line or shape on a slide.

2. Move the cursor over a point on the line or shape.

3. Wait until the cursor changes to a selection arrow with a star (see Figure 7-15), then click and drag to move the line or shape.

4. To nudge a line or shape horizontally or vertically, do one of the following:

   • Select the line or shape and press an arrow key to move in the direction of the arrow key.

   • Select a line or shape and press the Ctrl key and an arrow key to slightly nudge in the direction of the arrow key. The Ctrl key moves a line or object in smaller increments then when pressing just the arrow key.

Rotate Lines and Shapes

1. Create a line or shape on a slide.

2. Select the object to reveal its rotate handle and then move the cursor over the handle.

3. Wait until the cursor changes from a selection arrow to a semicircle and arrowhead (see Figure 7-16), then click and drag to rotate the line or shape.

 Drag left to rotate counterclockwise or right to rotate clockwise.

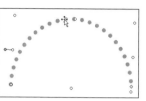

Figure 7-15: Position the cursor over a line and click and drag to move the line

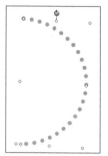

Figure 7-16: Drag left or right to rotate the object

Stack Lines and Shapes

1. Create a blank new slide.

2. Open the Drawing toolbar by choosing View⇨ Toolbars⇨Drawing.

3. Click the Line tool and draw a series of lines to create a map with lines intersecting.

 If you want to draw a freeform line, click the AutoShape button, select Lines from the drop-down menu, click the Curve line option (lower-left corner on the submenu), then draw a freeform shape with the line.

4. Press Ctrl+A or choose Edit⇨Select All to select all the lines.

5. Right-click and select Format AutoShape to open the Format AutoShape dialog box.

6. Choose 12 from the Weight drop-down menu for a 12-point line. Click OK to change all lines to 12 points (see Figure 7-17).

7. Press Control + A to select all the lines. Right click on a selected line and then select Grouping⇨Group to group the lines.

8. While the lines are selected, choose Edit⇨Copy.

9. Choose Edit⇨Paste.

10. Right-click and select Format AutoShape. The Format AutoShape dialog box opens.

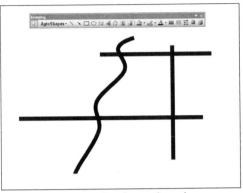

Figure 7-17: Intersecting lines forming the roads on a map

11. Choose 8 from the Weight drop-down menu.

12. Select White from the Color drop-down menu for the color.

13. Click OK.

14. Move the white lines to fit on top of the black 12-point lines by clicking and dragging or pressing the arrow keys (see Figure 7-18).

15. Import clip art or any images to enhance the appearance of your map by choosing Insert⇨Picture⇨Clip Art or choose From File to import an image.

16. Click the Text Box button on the Drawing toolbar and drag open a rectangle to create a text placeholder. Repeat, adding text placeholders as needed and type the text to describe the street names (see Figure 7-18).

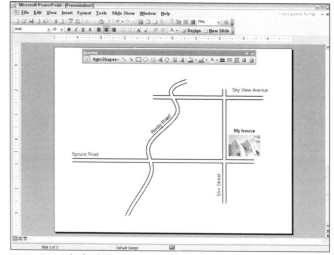

Figure 7-18: The finished map

Using Color, Texture, and Pattern

Color is an important element in communication. Each color has an inherent "personality" and can evoke emotion and action. Certain colors also have been historically associated with certain products, industries, and even messages. The colors you choose and the way you combine colors can have an effect on your presentation and the way it is perceived by your audience. You want to ensure that your color choices are never arbitrary but, instead, are well-thought-out.

Fortunately, PowerPoint makes choosing and using color simple. If you're not particularly color savvy, you can rest assured that PowerPoint's predefined color schemes are well designed. If you're feeling more creative, defining your own colors is easy. And if you decide color isn't enough, you also have the ability to add textures and patterns to your background and graphic elements. This chapter gives you the know-how to work with all three.

Chapter

8

Get ready to . . .

Apply a Color Scheme

1. Open a presentation in PowerPoint.

2. Choose Format⇨Slide Design to open the Slide Design task pane. You can also click Design in the Formatting toolbar.

3. Click Color Schemes at the top of the task pane.

4. Click the color scheme you want to use in the Apply a Color Scheme area, as shown in Figure 8-1. By default, the color scheme you choose is applied to all the slides in your presentation.

Apply a Color Scheme to Selected Slides

1. Open a presentation in PowerPoint.

2. Choose Format⇨Slide Design to open the Slide Design task pane. You can also click Design in the Formatting toolbar.

3. Click Color Schemes at the top of the task pane.

4. Click the Slides tab on the far left of the application window. If the Slides tab isn't visible, first choose View⇨Normal.

5. In the Slides tab area, Ctrl-click the slides whose current color scheme you want to change — while leaving the remaining slides unselected.

6. Hover your mouse over your desired color scheme in the Color Schemes area of the task pane. Click the downward-pointing arrow and select Apply to Selected Slides from the drop-down list, as shown in Figure 8-2.

 If you have applied more than one design template to your slides and want the color scheme applied to all slides, select Apply to All Slides from the drop-down list. If you want to apply the color scheme to a set of slides that use a particular design template, first select a slide in that group and then choose Apply to Master from the drop-down list.

Figure 8-1: Apply a color scheme to all of your slides

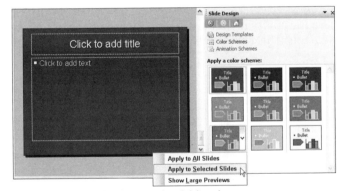

Figure 8-2: Apply a color scheme to selected slides only

Apply a Color Scheme to Notes Pages

1. Open a presentation in PowerPoint.

2. Choose Format⇨Slide Design to open the Slide Design task pane. You can also click Design in the Formatting toolbar.

3. Click Color Schemes at the top of the task pane.

4. If you want to apply a color scheme to one notes page only, select your desired slide in the Slides tab.

5. Choose View⇨Notes Page.

6. Hover your cursor over your desired color scheme in the Color Schemes area of the task pane. Click the downward-pointing arrow and select Apply to Notes Page from the drop-down list, as shown in Figure 8-3.

7. To apply the color scheme to all the notes pages, select Apply to All Notes Pages from the drop-down list.

Apply a Color Scheme to Handouts

1. Open a presentation in PowerPoint.

2. Choose Format⇨Slide Design to open the Slide Design task pane. You can also click Design in the Formatting toolbar.

3. Click Color Schemes at the top of the task pane.

4. Choose View⇨Master⇨Handout Master.

5. Hover your cursor over your desired color scheme in the Color Schemes area of the task pane. Click the downward-pointing arrow and select Apply to Handout Master from the drop-down list, as shown in Figure 8-4.

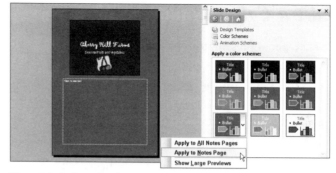

Figure 8-3: Apply a color scheme to notes pages

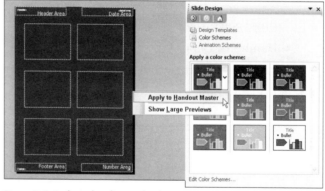

Figure 8-4: Apply a color scheme to handouts

Edit a Color Scheme

1. Open a presentation in PowerPoint.

2. Choose Format➪Slide Design to open the Slide Design task pane. You can also click Design in the Formatting toolbar.

3. Click Color Schemes at the top of the task pane.

4. Do one of the following to edit the color scheme of

   - **Slides:** Click the Slides tab on the far left of the application window, then Ctrl-click your desired slides.

   - **Notes:** Choose View➪Master➪Notes Master to edit the color scheme for all the notes pages. To change just a single notes page, select the slide in the Slides tab area.

   - **Handouts:** Choose View➪Master➪Handout Master.

5. Click Edit Color Schemes at the bottom of the task pane.

6. In the Edit Color Scheme dialog box, under the Custom tab, click the color you want to change in the Scheme colors area, as shown in Figure 8-5.

7. Click the Change Color button.

8. Do one of the following:

   - **Standard color palette:** Click the color you want. Click OK.

   - **Custom color palette:** Click with the crosshair icon to select a color, as shown in Figure 8-6. You can also drag the scroll bar to further fine tune the color. Click OK.

9. Repeat Steps 6, 7, and 8 for additional colors you want to modify.

10. Click Apply to modify the colors and exit the dialog box.

Figure 8-5: Select the colors you wish to modify

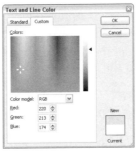

Figure 8-6: Select a new custom color for your scheme

 When you modify an existing color scheme, you automatically create a new one. It is added to the gallery in the Slide Design Color Schemes task pane for future use. To delete a color scheme, click the Delete Scheme button at the bottom of the Standard tab of the Edit Color Scheme dialog box (Step 8).

Use the Color Scheme from Another Presentation

1. Open both presentations in PowerPoint. (Choose Window⇨Arrange All to display your presentations side by side.)

2. In both presentations, click the Slides tab on the far left of the application window.

3. In the Slides tab area, select the slide in the first presentation that has the color scheme you want to use.

4. Click the Format Painter in the Formatting toolbar, then click the window of the second presentation. Finally, click the slide to which you want to apply the scheme, as shown in Figure 8-7.

Change the Slide Background Color

1. Open a presentation in PowerPoint.

2. Choose Format⇨Background.

3. In the Background dialog box, shown in Figure 8-8, click the downward-pointing arrow and select one of the eight colors from the current color scheme.

4. Click the Preview button to get a look at your modified background.

5. Click Apply to apply the new background color to selected slides only. Click Apply to All to apply the background to all slides.

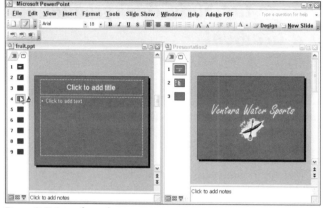

Figure 8-7: Copy schemes between two presentations

Figure 8-8: Change the background color of your slide(s)

To recolor multiple slides, *double-click* the Format Painter in the Formatting toolbar. Click the window of the second presentation. Then click each slide you want to apply the scheme to. When you're done with the Format Painter, press Esc to deselect the tool.

Change the Slide Background to a Gradient

1. Open a presentation in PowerPoint.

2. Choose Format⇨Background.

3. In the Background dialog box, click the downward-pointing arrow and select Fill Effects.

4. Click the Gradient tab.

5. Specify your color choices. Choose from One Color, Two Colors, or a Preset.

6. If you chose One Color in Step 5, first select your desired color from the Color 1 drop-down list. (Choose a color from the color scheme or click More Colors to access the Standard and Custom color palettes.) Use the slider below Color 1 to determine how dark or light you want your shading, as shown in Figure 8-9. The dark side fades your color to black; the light side fades your color to white. Finally, select your shading style.

7. If you chose Two Colors in Step 5, select your two desired colors from the Color 1 and Color 2 drop-down list. Then select your shading style.

8. If you chose Preset in Step 5, select your preset gradient from the drop-down list that appears. Then select your shading style.

9. Click OK to exit the Gradient dialog box.

10. Click Apply to apply the new background color to selected slides only, as shown in Figure 8-10. Click Apply to All to apply the background color to all slides.

Figure 8-9: Choose a one-color gradient

Figure 8-10: Change the background from solid to gradient

Change the Slide Background to a Texture

1. Open a presentation in PowerPoint.

2. Choose Format⇨Background.

3. In the Background dialog box, click the downward-pointing arrow and select Fill Effects.

4. Click the Texture tab of the Fill Effects dialog box, shown in Figure 8-11.

5. Select your desired texture from the default preset library. Or click Other Texture to select a file that you have found or created and have stored on your hard drive. Locate the file and then click the Insert button to import the file and close the Select Texture dialog box.

6. Click OK to exit the Texture dialog box.

7. Back in the Fill Effects dialog box, click Apply to apply the texture to selected slides only, as shown in Figure 8-13. Click Apply to All to apply the textured background to all slides.

 When using a texture or pattern as a background, be sure that your text is still legible and easily readable. Otherwise, your information won't get communicated to your audience.

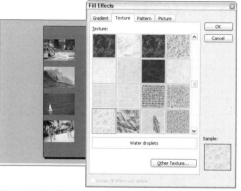

Figure 8-11: Choose a texture from the preset library

Figure 8-12: A water droplets texture applied to a Background

Change the Slide Background to a Pattern

1. Open a presentation in PowerPoint.

2. Choose Format⇨Background.

3. In the Background dialog box, click the downward-pointing arrow and select Fill Effects.

4. Click the Pattern tab, shown in Figure 8-13.

5. Select your desired pattern from the default preset library.

6. Select your desired foreground and background colors for the pattern. Choose a color from the color scheme or click More Colors to access the Standard and Custom color palettes.

7. Click OK to exit the Pattern dialog box.

8. Click Apply to apply the pattern to selected slides only, as shown in Figure 8-14, (Click Apply to All to apply the pattern background to all slides.)

 If you want to hide background graphics that are on the slide master, select the Omit Background Graphics from the Master option at the bottom of the Background dialog box.

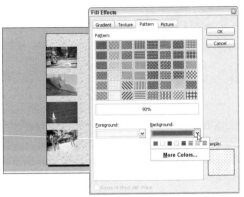

Figure 8-13: Choose a pattern from the preset library

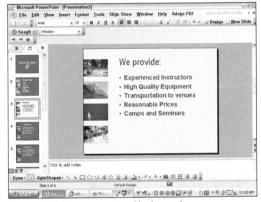

Figure 8-14: Your new patterned background

Change the Slide Background to an Image

1. Open a presentation in PowerPoint.

    Remember that, by default, when you change any background, the change applies to all slides that use the design template of the currently selected slide. If you want to change the background of only certain slides, select those slides in the Slide tab in Normal view.

2. Choose Format➪Background.

3. In the Background dialog box, click the downward-pointing arrow and select Fill Effects.

4. Click the Picture tab, shown in Figure 8-15.

5. Click Select Picture to select a file that you have found or created and have stored on your hard drive. Locate the file and then click the Insert button to import the file and close the Select Picture dialog box.

6. Click OK to exit the Picture dialog box.

7. Click Apply to apply the image to selected slides only, as shown in Figure 8-16. Click Apply to All to apply the image background to all slides.

Figure 8-15: Choose a picture for your background

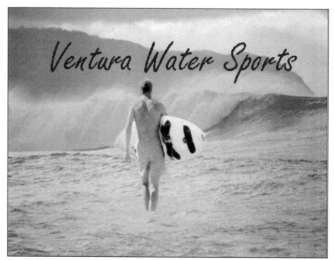

Figure 8-16: A picture enlivens a stale background

Change the Background of Notes

1. Open a presentation in PowerPoint.

2. Choose View⇨Notes Page.

3. Choose Format⇨Notes Background.

4. In the Notes Background dialog box, click the downward-pointing arrow and select one of the following:

    • **Automatic:** This option uses the background fill from the notes master.

    • **Other Color Scheme Colors:** Choose another scheme color, as shown in Figure 8-17.

    • **More Colors:** Choose a color from the Standard or Custom color palettes.

    • **Fill Effects:** Choose from Gradients, Textures, Patterns, or Pictures in the Fill Effects dialog box.

5. Click Apply to apply the new background to the current notes page only. Click Apply to All to apply the background to all notes pages.

Change the Background of Handouts

1. Open a presentation in PowerPoint.

2. Choose View⇨Master⇨Handout Master.

3. Choose Format⇨Handout Background.

4. In the Handout Background dialog box, click the arrow and select one of the options given.

5. Click Apply to apply the new background to all of the handouts, as shown in Figure 8-18.

Figure 8-17: Change the background of your notes pages

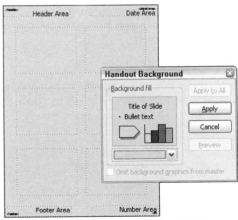

Figure 8-18: Change the background of your handouts

Add, Change, or Delete a Fill

1. Open a presentation in PowerPoint.

2. On your slide, select the AutoShape, picture, text box, or WordArt you want to modify.

3. On the Drawing toolbar, click the downward-pointing arrow next to the Fill Color icon, as shown in Figure 8-19. (If the Drawing toolbar is not visible, choose View⇨Toolbars⇨Drawing to display it onscreen.)

4. Select one of the following:

   - **No Fill:** This option removes any fill.

   - **Automatic:** This option uses the default fill color.

   - **Other Color Scheme Colors:** Choose one of the eight colors in the color scheme.

   - **More Colors:** Choose a color from the Standard or Custom color palettes.

   - **Fill Effects:** Choose from Gradients, Textures, Patterns, or Pictures in the Fill Effects dialog box. For details on these options, see this chapter's previous sections about changing slide backgrounds.

5. The element you chose in Step 2 should have a new fill, as shown in Figure 8-20.

 To change the color of a line, simply double-click the line on the slide. In the Format AutoShapes dialog box, choose your desired color from the drop-down list in the Line area.

Figure 8-19: Add a fill to an AutoShape, text box, picture, or WordArt

Figure 8-20: A text box gains a colored fill

Change the Color of Text

1. Open a presentation in PowerPoint.

2. On your slide, select the text whose color you want to modify.

3. On either the Drawing or Formatting toolbar, click the downward-pointing arrow next to the Font Color icon, as shown in Figure 8-21.

4. Select one of the following:

   • **Automatic:** This option uses the default fill color.

   • **Other Color Scheme Colors:** Choose one of the eight colors in the color scheme.

   • **More Colors:** Choose a color from the Standard or Custom color palettes.

5. The text color is changed, as shown in Figure 8-22

 To change the color of lines or AutoShapes, see Chapter 5.

Figure 8-21: Choose your desired font color

Figure 8-22: Your text is recolored

Change the Color or Fill of Text in WordArt

1. Open a presentation in PowerPoint.

2. On your slide, select the WordArt whose color you want to modify.

3. On the WordArt toolbar, click the Format WordArt icon, as shown in Figure 8-23.

4. In the Format WordArt dialog box, click the Colors and Lines tab.

5. In the Fill section, choose a color from the drop-down list, as shown in Figure 8-24:

   - **No Fill:** This option removes any fill.

   - **Automatic:** This option uses the default fill color.

   - **Other Color Scheme Colors:** Choose one of the eight colors in the color scheme.

   - **More Colors:** Choose a color from the Standard or Custom color palettes.

   - **Fill Effects:** Choose from Gradients, Textures, Patterns, or Pictures in the Fill Effects dialog box. For details on these options, see this chapter's previous sections about changing slide backgrounds.

6. The WordArt text color is changed.

 You can also change the color of the WordArt border by specifying a color in the Line area of the Format WordArt dialog box.

Figure 8-23: Click the Format WordArt icon

Figure 8-24: Choose your desired new color in the WordArt dialog box

Working with Pictures

*T*he old adage, "A picture is worth a thousand words," is certainly true when it comes to presentations. Visually conveying information with images rather than words is often quicker, has more impact, and is more interesting.

Working with pictures in PowerPoint is easy. You can import a variety of file types by using a variety of methods. You can import scanned TIFFs from your scanner or import JPEGS from your digital camera. If you don't have access to either of these devices, you can import clip art and photographs from stock agencies. Or just use the multitude of art available within PowerPoint's libraries, which include 140,000 pieces of clip art, photos, animations, and sounds. After you have a picture, you can easily modify its size, position, and even contrast and color to suit your needs. This chapter gives you all the information necessary to work with pictures of all sorts.

Chapter 9

Get ready to . . .

Insert a Picture from Clip Art

1. Open a presentation in PowerPoint.

2. Choose Insert⇨Picture⇨Clip Art to open the Clip Art task pane. You can also click the Insert Clip Art icon on the Drawing toolbar.

3. In the Search For box, enter a keyword that describes the art you are looking for.

4. In the Search In box, select the collections from the drop-down list that you want PowerPoint to search in for your art. You can choose Everywhere (all collections), My Collections (clips you have stored on your hard drive), Office Collections (clips that are part of the Office suite), and Web Collections (clips located on the Web).

5. In the Results Should Be box, select your desired media type from the drop-down list. Choose from Clip Art, Photographs, Movies, and Sounds. For specific file formats under each media type, click the plus sign to expand the directory.

6. Click the Go button.

7. In the Results box, click the thumbnail of your desired clip. It will then be inserted into your slide, as shown in Figure 9-1. To find similar clips (if the clip has a defined style), click the downward-pointing arrow on the right of the clip and select Find Similar Style from the pop-up list. Note that you can also insert, copy, or delete clips from this pop-up list.

Figure 9-1: Insert clip art into your slide

 For search keywords, you can also enter all or part of the file name of the art. If you don't know the exact name, you can use a question mark to substitute for a single character in a name or use an asterisk to substitute for multiple characters in the name. If you type two words, such as **yellow leaves**, in the Search For box, PowerPoint will search for clips using the keywords *yellow* and *leaves*. If you type in two words enclosed by quotation marks, such as **"yellow leaves"**, the program will search for clips that contain the phrase *yellow leaves*. And if you type in two words separated by a comma, such as **yellow, leaves**, PowerPoint will search for clips with the keywords *yellow* or *leaves*.

 The Clip Organizer holds your clips. Clips include clip art, photos, sounds, and videos. In addition to the Office clips that automatically reside in the Clip Organizer, you can access Office clips on the Web. You can also import and store your own clips in the Clip Organizer. Use this powerful tool to organize, find, and insert your clips.

Insert a Picture from a File

1. Open a presentation in PowerPoint.

2. Click the slide where you want the picture to appear. If you want the picture to appear on multiple slides or title slides, add it to the slide master or title master, respectively.

3. Choose Insert⇔Picture⇔From File. You can also click the Insert Picture icon on the Drawing toolbar.

4. In the Insert Picture dialog box, navigate to your desired file.

5. To embed the file into your PowerPoint presentation, click Insert, as shown in Figure 9-2. To link the file to your PowerPoint presentation, click the downward-pointing arrow next to Insert and select Link to File. The picture is inserted into your slide, as shown in Figure 9-3.

 Embedded pictures become part of the presentation file. They do not change within the presentation file even if the picture is changed in its source program. Linked pictures do *not* become part of the presentation. The presentation only stores the location for the link and displays a proxy (a representation) of the picture. The picture will change within the presentation if it is modified in its source program.

Figure 9-2: Choose whether to embed or link your picture

Figure 9-3: A picture inserted into a slide

Insert a Picture from a Scanner or Camera

1. Open a presentation in PowerPoint.

2. If you are scanning an image, set it up on the scanner.

3. Select Insert⇨Picture⇨From Scanner or Camera.

4. If you have multiple devices connected to your computer, choose the device you are using under Device. You can also click the Insert Picture icon on the Drawing toolbar.

5. If you selected a scanner, choose either Web Quality (low resolution) or Print Quality (high resolution). Click Insert to scan your picture. If you want to customize your settings, click Custom Insert. Note that if the Insert button is grayed out, your particular scanning software does not support an automatic scan. Click Custom Insert instead, as shown in Figure 9-4. Proceed with scanning your image using your scanning software.

6. If you selected a digital camera, click Custom Insert. Locate the image on your camera, select it, and click Insert. If PowerPoint doesn't recognize your camera, your computer might treat your camera as a removable drive. If that's the case, choose Insert⇨Picture⇨From File and locate your camera in the Insert Picture dialog box.

7. The picture will then be inserted into your slide, as shown in Figure 9-5.

 Click Organize Clips at the bottom of the Clip Art task pane to add, rearrange, or delete clips from your collections.

Figure 9-4: Click Custom Insert if your device is a digital camera

Figure 9-5: A picture inserted from a digital camera

Add a Clip to the Clip Organizer

1. Open a presentation in PowerPoint.

2. Choose Insert⇨Picture⇨Clip Art to open the Clip Art task pane. You can also click the Insert Clip Art icon on the Drawing toolbar.

3. At the bottom of the Clip Art task pane, click the Organize Clips link, shown in Figure 9-6.

4. In the Clip Organizer dialog box, choose File⇨Add Clips to Organizer⇨On My Own.

5. Locate and select the file you want to add.

6. Click Add To and select the collection you want to add the clip to, as shown in Figure 9-7, or click Add to add it to your Favorites folder. Click New to create a new collection.

7. Close the Clip Organizer dialog box.

 You can also save pictures, WordArt, and AutoShapes you created in PowerPoint. Select the object and choose Edit⇨Copy. Select your desired collections folder and choose Edit⇨Paste.

Figure 9-6: Use the Clip Organizer to store clips

Figure 9-7: Store clips in the folder of your choice

Insert Pictures to Create a Photo Album

1. Choose Insert⇨Picture⇨New Photo Album. Note that when you insert pictures to create a Photo Album, PowerPoint creates a new presentation. Any other open presentations will be untouched. Also note that a title slide is automatically created for you when you create a new photo album, as shown in Figure 9-8.

   You can also create a new photo album by clicking New⇨Photo Album in the New Presentation task pane.

2. In the Format Photo Album dialog box, add the images you want in your album. You can insert pictures from files on your hard drive, from or removable media or from a scanner or digital camera, as shown in Figure 9-9. For details on either task, see the previous sections in this chapter.

3. To insert text boxes, which will show up on their own separate slides, click the New Text Box button.

4. Rearrange the order of any of your photos and text boxes by clicking the up and down arrows directly under the Pictures in Album list.

5. Remove any unwanted images or text boxes by selecting them in the list and clicking the Remove button. This removes the pictures from the album only; it doesn't delete them from the computer or other source.

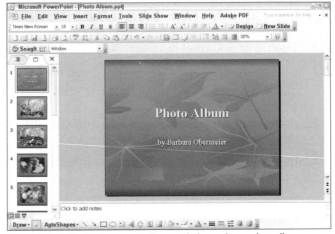

Figure 9-8: A title slide is automatically created when making a photo album

Figure 9-9: Insert images into your photo album

6. Fix any images, as follows:

   - **Rotate:** Click the Rotate Left or Rotate Right buttons under the Preview thumbnail.

   - **Contrast:** Click the More Contrast or Less Contrast buttons under the Preview thumbnail.

   - **Brightness:** Click the More Brightness or Less Brightness buttons under the Preview thumbnail.

7. Specify your photo album options, as follows:

   - **Captions below ALL pictures:** Filenames will appear under each photo.

   - **ALL pictures black and white:** All images will be converted from color to grayscale or black and white.

   - **Picture Layout:** Fit to Slide displays your image across the entire slide. You do not have access to frame options or design templates.

   - **Frame shape:** Choose the shape of your picture frame. Choose from shapes such as rounded rectangle and oval.

   - **Design template:** You may choose a design template to use in your photo album presentation. Click the Browse button and choose your desired template from the dialog box. Click Select.

8. Click the Create button.

9. PowerPoint creates your new photo album, as shown in Figure 9-10.

Figure 9-10: A photo album presentation

 To modify your photo album, choose Format➪Photo Album.

Recolor Clip Art

1. Open a presentation in PowerPoint.

2. Select the clip art whose color you want to change.

3. Choose View⇨Toolbars⇨Picture.

4. Click the Recolor Picture button on the Picture toolbar.

5. In the Recolor Picture dialog box, select Colors to change any color in the clip art. Select Fills to change only background or fill colors in the clip art.

6. Select an original color in the clip art, as shown in Figure 9-11. Then select the color you want to change it to from the drop-down list. Click More Colors to access colors in the Standard or Custom color palettes.

7. Click the Preview button to see the color changes on the slide.

8. Click OK to exit the dialog box. Your clip art is recolored, as shown in Figure 9-12.

 Want more control over changing your colors? If you inserted a Windows Metafile (.wmf) from the Clipboard, first convert it into a drawing object by right-clicking the clip art. Choose Edit Picture. Click Yes in the dialog box. Use the tools on the Drawing toolbar to modify the individual components of the clip art. Note that you cannot modify bitmap, JPEG, GIF, PNG, or TIFF files. These can be modified only in an image-editing program.

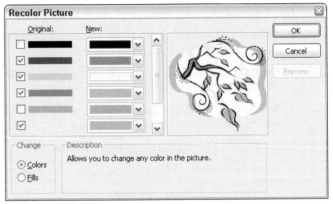

Figure 9-11: Select colors to change in your clip art

Figure 9-12: Clip art color changed

Resize a Picture Manually

1. Open a presentation in PowerPoint.

2. Select the picture you want to resize. You can also resize AutoShapes and WordArt.

3. Position your mouse cursor over one of the handles surrounding the picture, as shown in Figure 9-13.

4. Drag the handle toward or away from the center to resize the picture smaller or larger. Remember to hold the Shift key down while you drag to keep the picture's original proportions. To keep the center of the object in the same place, press the Ctrl key while you drag.

Resize a Picture Precisely

1. Open a presentation in PowerPoint.

2. Select the picture you want to resize. You can also resize AutoShapes and WordArt.

3. Choose Format⇨Picture (or AutoShapes).

4. Click the Size tab in the Format Picture dialog box, shown in Figure 9-13.

5. Enter your desired size in the Height and Width boxes. Or enter your desired scale percentage in the Height and Width boxes.

6. Select the Lock Aspect Ratio option to keep the picture's original proportions.

Figure 9-13: Resize a picture by dragging a handle
Photo Credit: PhotoSpin

Figure 9-14: Resize a picture by entering dimensions
Photo Credit: PhotoSpin

Crop a Picture

1. Open a presentation in PowerPoint.

2. Select the picture you want to crop. You can also resize AutoShapes and WordArt.

     Cropping is one of the easiest things you can do to improve the composition of your pictures and home in on the focal point.

3. Choose View➪Toolbars➪Picture.

4. Click the Crop button on the Picture toolbar.

5. Position your cursor over a cropping handle and drag, as shown in Figure 9-15. To crop equally on two sides simultaneously, press the Ctrl key as you drag the center crop handle on a side.

6. Click anywhere in your slide outside the selected picture to deselect the Crop tool.

Flip or Rotate a Picture

1. Open a presentation in PowerPoint.

2. Select the picture you want to flip or rotate. You can also flip or rotate AutoShapes and WordArt.

3. Choose View➪Toolbars➪Drawing.

4. On the Drawing toolbar, click Draw and then select Rotate or Flip.

5. Select Free Rotate, Rotate Left 90°, Rotate Right 90°, or Flip Horizontal or Flip Vertical, as shown in Figure 9-16.

6. If you selected Free Rotate in Step 5, position your cursor over a handle and drag.

Figure 9-15: Crop a picture
Photo Credit: PhotoSpin

Figure 9-16: Rotate or flip your pictures
Photo Credit: PhotoSpin

 You can also simply select the object, position your cursor over the green handle, and drag. If you don't see the rotate handle, then rotate via the Drawing toolbar.

Align and Distribute Pictures

1. Open a presentation in PowerPoint.

2. Select the pictures you want to align. You can also align and distribute AutoShapes and WordArt.

3. Choose View⇨Toolbars⇨Drawing.

4. On the Drawing toolbar, click Draw and then select Align or Distribute, as shown in Figure 9-17.

5. You can align and distribute pictures relative to the slide or relative to each other. If you want to align and distribute relative to the slide, select the Relative to Slide option first. Then click Draw again and choose your alignment and distribution method.

6. Select your desired alignment or distribution method from the submenu. Note that the icons visually show each method.

Group Pictures

1. Open a presentation in PowerPoint.

2. Select the pictures you want to group. You can also group AutoShapes and WordArt.

3. Choose View⇨Toolbars⇨Drawing.

4. On the Drawing toolbar, click Draw and then select Group, as shown in Figure 9-18.

5. Your selected pictures are now grouped.

 If you have meticulously aligned and distributed numerous photos, you may want to group them to retain their precise alignment and spacing.

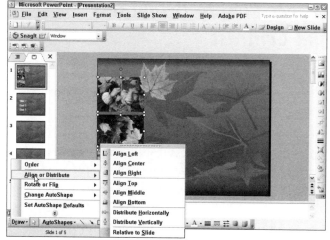

Figure 9-17: Align and distribute your pictures
Photo Credit: PhotoSpin

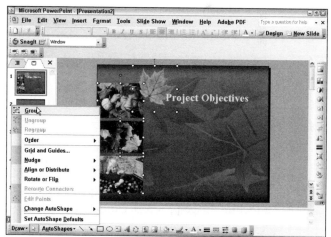

Figure 9-18: Group pictures to keep them together
Photo Credit: PhotoSpin

Adjust Picture Brightness and Contrast

1. Open a presentation in PowerPoint.

2. Select a picture that needs a brightness or contrast adjustment.

3. Choose View⇨Toolbars⇨Picture.

4. Click the More or Less Contrast buttons on the Picture toolbar to adjust the contrast of the image.

5. Click the More or Less Brightness buttons on the Picture toolbar to adjust the brightness of the image.

6. Your picture's contrast and/or brightness is adjusted, as shown in Figure 9-19.

Adjust Picture Color

1. Open a presentation in PowerPoint.

2. Select a picture that needs a color adjustment.

3. Choose View⇨Toolbars⇨Picture.

4. Click the Color button on the Picture toolbar.

5. Choose from

   Automatic: Reverts the picture back to its default color

   Grayscale: Converts the picture to a grayscale image

   Black and White: Converts the picture to a black-and-white image (2 levels, either black or white)

   Washout: Desaturates the image

6. Your picture's color is adjusted, as shown in Figure 9-20.

Figure 9-19: Adjust the brightness and contrast in a picture
Photo Credit: PhotoSpin

Figure 9-20: Adjust the color of a picture
Photo Credit: PhotoSpin

Add Transparency to a Picture

1. Open a presentation in PowerPoint.

2. Select the picture you want to add transparency to. You can add transparency to bitmap images and some clip art.

3. Choose View⇨Toolbars⇨Picture.

4. Click the Set Transparent Color button on the Picture toolbar.

5. Click the color you want to make transparent.

6. That area becomes transparent, as shown in Figure 9-21.

Compress a Picture to Reduce File Size

1. Open a presentation in PowerPoint.

2. Select View⇨Toolbars⇨Picture.

3. Click the Compress Picture button on the Picture toolbar.

4. Select your desired options, as shown in Figure 9-22:

   - **Apply to:** Select whether you want to compress selected pictures or all pictures in your presentation.

   - **Resolution:** Choose the resolution that is appropriate for your desired medium — print or the Web.

   - **Compress Pictures:** Compresses the picture information to create a smaller file.

   - **Delete cropped areas of pictures:** Deletes areas of the pictures that were hidden during cropping.

5. Click OK in the Compress Pictures dialog box.

Figure 9-21: Add transparency to your pictures
Photo Credit: PhotoSpin

Figure 9-22: Compressing pictures makes file sizes smaller

 Compressing pictures shrinks their file sizes and allows them to download from the Web faster.

Add Shadows

1. Open a presentation in PowerPoint.

2. Select the AutoShape(s), text, or picture to which you wish to add a shadow effect.

3. Choose View➪Toolbars➪Drawing.

4. Click the Shadow Style button on the Drawing toolbar.

5. Click the shadow style you want from the pop-up palette, as shown in Figure 9-23.

6. To change the specific settings of that shadow, such as position or color, select Shadow Settings, as shown in Figure 9-24.

7. Your shadow is placed, as shown in Figure 9-25. To remove the Shadow, select No Shadow.

 To change a shadow back to its default color settings, choose Automatic in the Shadow Color drop-down palette under Shadow Settings.

Figure 9-23: Choose your desired shadow style

Figure 9-24: Change your shadow settings

Figure 9-25: Shadows add a subtle depth

Creating Tables and Graphs

Data is often grasped more quickly and with more understanding and impact when it's presented in a simple, organized, and visual way. In PowerPoint, tables and graphs are a couple of ways to more effectively present data, especially quantitative, complex, or tedious data. This chapter describes the powerful options within PowerPoint to work with graphs and tables. Tables and graphs can be created from scratch within PowerPoint or imported from Microsoft Word or Microsoft Excel.

After your data has been entered into a table or graph, PowerPoint provides the ability to modify virtually all the elements, from modifying a table's font, columns and rows, borders, and shading to adding fill effects. You can even insert your favorite picture in a table cell. If you've created one of the many types of graphs, PowerPoint provides the ability to alter almost all the graph objects by modifying a graph's type, font, axis, grid, borders, shading, labels, legend, and fill effects.

Chapter 10

Get ready to . . .

Insert a Table from Scratch

1. Open a presentation in PowerPoint.

2. In Normal view, under the Slides tab, select the slide on which you want to insert a table.

3. Choose Insert⇨Table. You can also click the Insert Table button on the Standard toolbar.

4. In the Insert Table dialog box, shown in Figure 10-1, select your desired number of columns and rows for the table. Click OK. Your table appears on the slide. To enter data, see "Enter Table Text," later in this chapter.

Insert a Table from a Layout

1. Open a presentation in PowerPoint.

2. In Normal view, under the Slides tab, select the slide on which you want to insert a table.

3. Choose View⇨Task Pane, if it isn't visible.

4. Choose Slide Layout from the Task Pane drop-down menu. Scroll down to Other Layouts and double-click the Title and Table layout, as shown in Figure 10-2.

5. Double-click the table icon on the slide to open the Insert Table dialog box.

6. In the Insert Table dialog box, select your desired number of columns and rows for the table. Click OK. Your table appears on the slide. To enter data, see "Enter Table Text," later in this chapter.

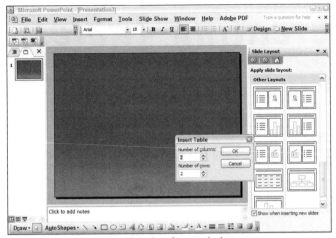

Figure 10-1: Enter your desired number of rows and columns

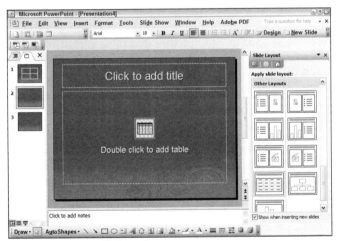

Figure 10-2: Insert a table from a layout

Insert a Table by Drawing

1. Open a presentation in PowerPoint.

2. In Normal view, under the Slides tab, select the slide on which you want to insert a table.

3. Choose View⇨Toolbars⇨Tables and Borders.

4. To display a grid on the slide, choose View⇨Grid and Guides. You can also click the Show/Hide Grid button on the Standard toolbar.

5. In the Grid and Guides dialog box, shown in Figure 10-3, enter your desired grid spacing. Check the Display Grid on Screen option and click OK.

6. Click the Draw Table button (first button on the left) on the Tables and Borders toolbar. The cursor changes into a pencil icon.

7. Click and drag diagonally across the table to define the outside border of the table. Release the mouse when you have your desired table shape.

8. Next, draw your desired table rows and columns, as shown in Figure 10-4. To enter data, see "Enter Table Text," later in this chapter.

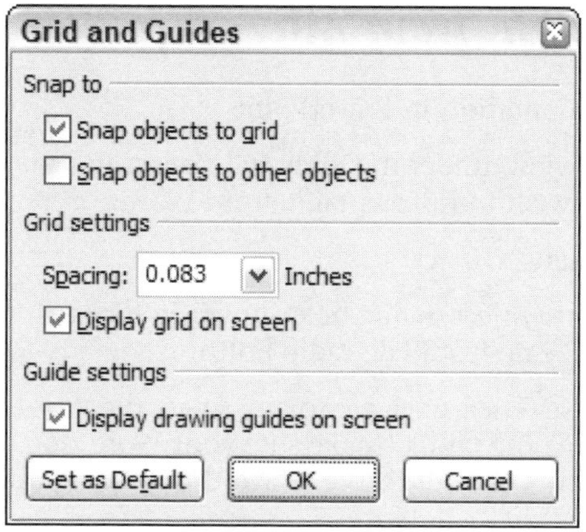

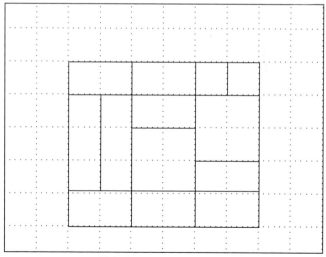

Figure 10-3: Grid and Guides dialog box

Figure 10-4: Create a table by drawing

Insert a Table from Microsoft Word

1. Open a presentation in PowerPoint.

2. In Normal view, under the Slides tab, select the slide on which you wish to insert a table from Word.

3. Choose Insert⇨Object.

4. In the Insert Object dialog box, shown in Figure 10-5, select the Create from File radio button.

5. Click Browse. Then navigate to and select the Word file that contains the table. (Make sure your Word document contains only the table to avoid importing unnecessary text.) Click OK twice.

6. Your table is inserted on the slide, as shown in Figure 10-6. Resize the table by dragging a corner sizing handle; click and drag the table to reposition it. To enter data, see "Enter Table Text," later in this chapter.

 Double-click the Word table, and a Word window will open within your PowerPoint slide so that you can edit the table or apply PowerPoint formatting commands. The original Word file will not change.

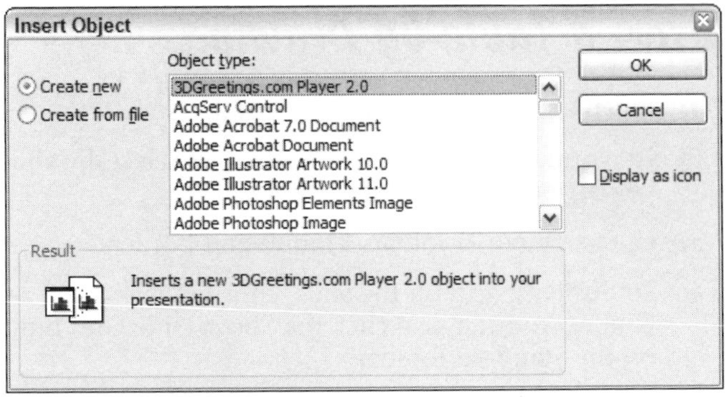

Figure 10-5: Navigate to your Word file

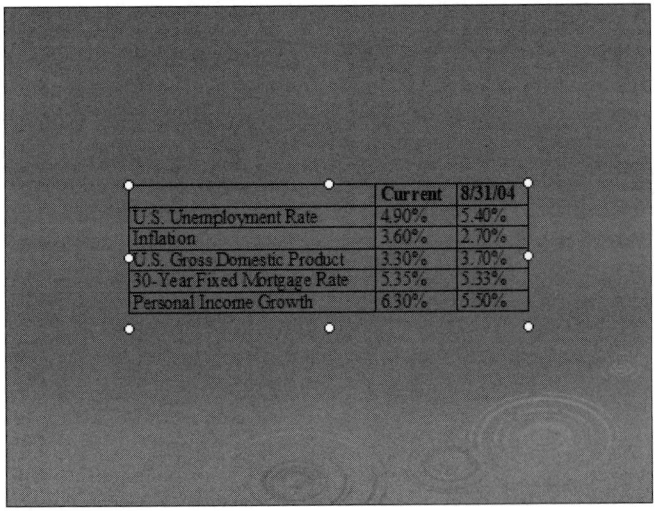

Figure 10-6: A table inserted from Word

Enter Table Text

1. Open a presentation in PowerPoint.

2. In Normal view, under the Slides tab, select the slide that contains the table you want to modify.

3. Select a cell by clicking it and then type your desired text, as shown in Figure 10-7. If you type to the end of the cell, the text automatically wraps to the next line.

4. Press Tab to advance to the next cell to the right. If you are at the end of the row, you advance to the first cell in the next row.

5. Press Enter to insert another line within a cell.

6. Press Ctrl+Tab to insert a tab within a cell.

 Press the up-arrow or down-arrow key to move up or down in a column.

Format Table Text

1. Open a presentation in PowerPoint.

2. In Normal view, under the Slides tab, select the slide that contains the table you want to format.

3. Highlight your text within the cell, row, or column.

4. Choose Format➪Font.

5. In the Font dialog box, shown in Figure 10-8, enter your desired font type, style, size, effects, or color. Click Preview to check out your formatting before accepting the changes. Click OK.

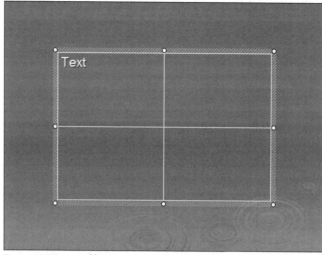

Figure 10-7: Insert table text

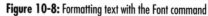

Figure 10-8: Formatting text with the Font command

 Formatting commands in the Formatting toolbar allow you to change text alignment (left, center, or right).

Add and Modify Table Columns and Rows

1. Open a presentation in PowerPoint.

2. In Normal view, under the Slides tab, select the slide that contains the table you want to modify.

3. To add a row, click in the row above or below where the new row is to be inserted.

4. On the Tables and Borders toolbar, choose Table➪Insert Rows Above or Table➪Insert Rows Below, as shown in Figure 10-9.

5. To add a column, click in the column to the left or to the right of where the new column is to be inserted. On the Tables and Borders toolbar, choose Table➪Insert Columns to the Left or Table➪Insert Columns to the Right, as shown in Figure 10-9. Figure 10-10 shows the extra column inserted.

 You can also click the row or column next to the point where you want to insert a new one. Then right-click and select Insert Rows or Insert Columns from the context menu. A new row is inserted above the selected row, or a new column is added to the left of the selected column.

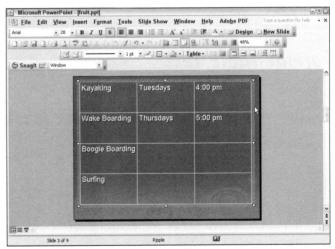

Figure 10-9: Use the Table menu to add a new row or column

Figure 10-10: Adding an extra column to a table

6. To change the size of any row, first click outside the table to deselect any cells.

7. Position the pointer on the lower border of the row to be modified. Your cursor changes to a double-headed arrow, as shown in Figure 10-11.

8. Click and drag the border up or down to increase or decrease the height.

 To change the height of all rows evenly, click anywhere on the table to select it and then click the Distribute Rows Evenly button in the Tables and Borders toolbar. The rows will be set to the same height, and the content will adjust to fit.

9. To change the width of any column, first click outside the table to deselect any cells.

10. Position the pointer on the right border of the column to be modified. With the double-headed arrow cursor, click and drag the border to the left or right to increase or decrease the width.

 To let PowerPoint set the column width to the widest entry within the column, position the pointer on the right border of the column to be modified and double-click with the double-headed arrow cursor. To change the size of all columns evenly, click anywhere on the table to select it and then click the Distribute Columns Evenly button in the Tables and Borders toolbar. The Columns will be set to the same width, and the content will adjust to fit.

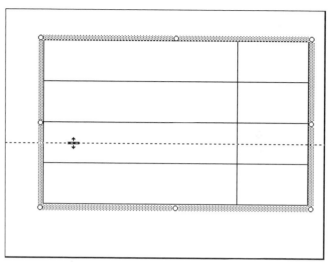

Figure 10-11: Changing row height by dragging a border

 Delete borders by using the Eraser tool, found in the Tables and Borders toolbar. Just click the border you wish to erase.

Modify Table Borders

1. Open a presentation in PowerPoint.

2. In Normal view, under the Slides tab, select the slide that contains the table you want to modify.

3. Choose View⇨Toolbars⇨Tables and Borders.

4. Click the edge of the table to select the entire table. Note that if you click inside a cell, only the cell borders will be formatted.

5. In the Tables and Borders toolbar, choose Table⇨Borders and Fill.

6. In the Format Table dialog box, shown in Figure 10-12, select the Borders tab. Specify your border style, width, and color. Using the diagram or buttons, specify which borders you want to modify.

7. Click the Preview button to view your modifications before accepting them.

 You can also change borders by utilizing the Border Style, Border Width, and Border Color drop-down palettes on the Tables and Borders toolbar, shown in Figure 10-13. Select the desired border style, width, and color. Your cursor changes to a pencil icon. Click any border to apply the settings (press Esc to deselect the pencil icon). Or select your desired border configuration from the Borders drop-down list.

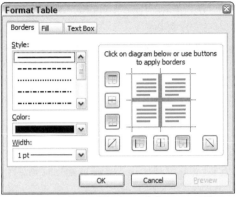

Figure 10-12: Change all borders with the Format Table dialog box

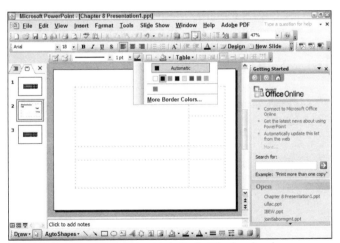

Figure 10-13: Change border color with the Border Color drop-down box

Shade the Table, Cells, Columns, or Rows

1. Open a presentation in PowerPoint.

2. In Normal view, under the Slides tab, select the slide that contains the table you want to modify.

3. Choose View➪Toolbars➪Tables and Borders.

4. Select the entire table by clicking the edge of the table. To select a single cell, simply click inside that cell. To select a group of cells, drag your cursor through your desired cells.

5. In the Tables and Borders toolbar, click Fill Color and choose your desired color, as shown in Figure 10-14. Click More Fill Colors to choose from additional colors.

Apply Fill Effects to a Table

1. Open a presentation in PowerPoint.

2. In Normal view, under the Slides tab, select the slide that contains the table you want to add a fill effect to.

3. Choose View➪Toolbars➪Tables and Borders.

4. Select the table, row, column, or cell to which you want to apply the fill effect.

5. In the Tables and Borders toolbar, click Fill Color and, from the drop-down list that appears, choose Fill Effects.

6. In the Fill Effects dialog box, shown in Figure 10-15, click the Gradient, Texture, or Pattern tab. Select the desired effects. Click the Preview button to see how your fill effect will appear in your table. Then click OK.

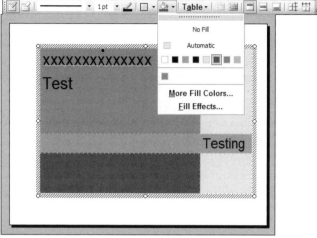

Figure 10-14: Shade a table selection by using the Fill Color feature

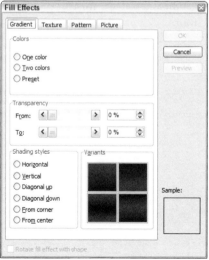

Figure 10-15: Apply a gradient, texture, or pattern to your table

Insert Pictures into a Table

1. Open a presentation in PowerPoint.

2. In Normal view, under the Slides tab, select the slide that contains the table you want to insert a picture into.

3. Choose View⇨Toolbars⇨Tables and Borders.

4. Select the table, row, column, or cell into which you want to insert a picture.

5. In the Tables and Borders toolbar, click Fill Color, and from the drop-down list, choose Fill Effects.

6. In the Fill Effects dialog box, click the Picture tab.

7. Click Select Picture.

8. In the Select Picture dialog box, shown in Figure 10-16, navigate to and select the picture you want to insert.

9. Click Insert. Click Preview to get a look at how it will appear in your table.

10. Click OK. The picture appears in your table, as shown in Figure 10-17.

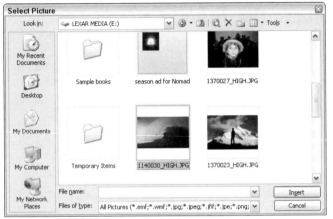

Figure 10-16: Insert pictures into a table

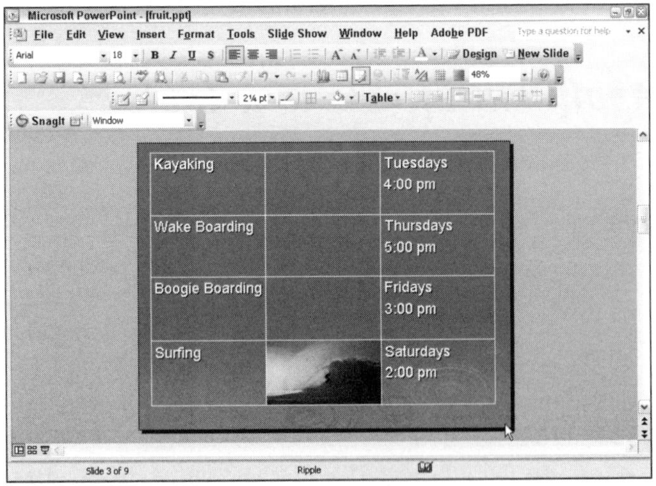

Figure 10-17: A picture adds visual interest to a table
Photo Credit: PhotoSpin

Enter Formulas with Microsoft Equation 3.0

1. Open a presentation in PowerPoint.

2. In Normal view, under the Slides tab, select the slide onto which you wish to enter an equation. Equations are for display purposes only. No calculations take place.

3. Choose Insert➪Object.

4. In the Insert Object dialog box, select Create new.

5. Scroll down to Microsoft Equation 3.0. Select it and click OK.

6. The Equation Editor dialog box appears, as shown in Figure 10-18.

7. From the bottom-row toolbar, select a template. From the top-row toolbar, click the symbols you need and type the text required to complete the formula. Close the Equation Editor window. The equation appears on the slide as shown in Figure 10-19. Drag the equation to position it on the slide.

Use the sizing handles to resize the selected equation. To edit a formula that you've already created, double-click the equation to reopen the Equation Editor.

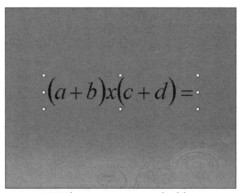

Figure 10-18: Insert Formulas with Microsoft Equation 3.0

$$(a+b)x(c+d)=$$

Figure 10-19: The equation appears on the slide

Create a Graph from Scratch

1. Open a presentation in PowerPoint, and in Normal view, under the Slides tab, select the slide on which you want to insert a graph.

2. Choose Insert⇨Chart. A huge Microsoft Graph window containing a default chart and an associated sample datasheet appears, as shown in Figure 10-20.

3. Enter your data into the datasheet as required. For details, see "Enter Data into the Datasheet," later in this chapter. Close the datasheet.

4. Click anywhere outside the chart border to exit Microsoft Graph and return to your slide.

 Use the sizing handles to resize the graph. Drag to reposition the chart. To edit a chart that you've already created, double-click the chart to reopen the Microsoft Graph window.

Import an Excel Spreadsheet or Graph

1. Open a presentation in PowerPoint, and in Normal view, under the Slides tab, select the slide on which you want to place the Excel spreadsheet.

2. Choose Insert⇨Object.

3. In the Insert Object dialog box, select Create from File.

4. Click the Browse button. In the Browse dialog box, locate and select the Excel file to be imported and then click OK twice.

5. The Excel spreadsheet or graph is imported onto the slide, as shown in Figure 10-21.

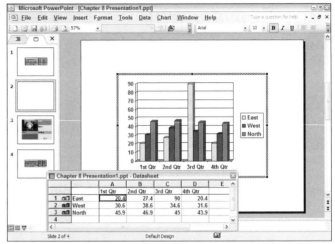

Figure 10-20: Insert a default chart onto a slide

Figure 10-21: Import an Excel spreadsheet onto a slide

Enter Data into the Datasheet

1. Open a presentation in PowerPoint.

2. In Normal view, under the Slides tab, select the slide containing the graph datasheet to be edited.

3. Double-click the graph. Microsoft Graph appears, along with the graph and associated datasheet, as shown in Figure 10-22.

4. Double-click the datasheet cell to be edited and change the values as needed.

5. To finish, click anywhere outside the chart border.

Select a Graph Type

1. Open a presentation in PowerPoint.

2. In Normal view, under the Slides tab, select the slide containing the graph to be modified.

3. Double-click the graph. Microsoft Graph appears, along with the graph and associated datasheet.

4. Choose Chart⇨Chart Type. In the Chart Type dialog box, shown in Figure 10-23, select your desired type from the Chart type list and then select your desired type from the Chart subtype palette on the right. Click the Press and Hold to View Sample button to see how your data looks in the particular chart type.

5. To finish, click OK.

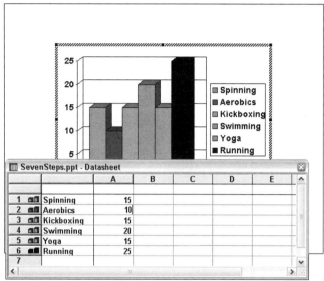

Figure 10-22: Enter data into the graph datasheet

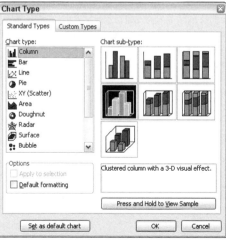

Figure 10-23: Select a chart type

Format a Graph's Text

1. Open a presentation in PowerPoint.

2. In Normal view, under the Slides tab, select the slide that contains the graph to be modified.

3. Double-click the graph. Microsoft Graph appears, along with the graph and associated datasheet.

4. Right-click anywhere on the open chart area (away from text or numbers), as shown in Figure 10-24, and choose Format Chart Area from the context menu. You can also double-click anywhere on the open chart area.

5. In the Format Chart Area dialog box, click the Font tab.

6. Modify the font size, color, type, style, and effect, as shown in Figure 10-25.

7. Click OK.

 Your chart consists of several components that are enclosed within the chart area, as indicated by the border that appears when you select the chart. The area that contains your axes, values, grid lines, and symbols such as bars, pie, and lines (depending on your chart type) is referred to as the *plot area*. The *legend area* explains the symbols used in the chart. To find out what other individual chart components are called, simply hover you mouse over the item to view a description.

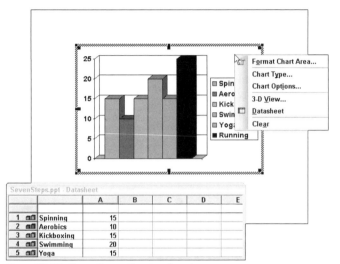

Figure 10-24: Choose Format Chart Area from the context menu

Figure 10-25: Modify the text of a graph

Format a Graph's Title and Legend

1. Open a presentation in PowerPoint.

2. In Normal view, under the Slides tab, select the slide that contains the graph to be modified.

3. Double-click the graph. Microsoft Graph appears, along with the graph and associated datasheet.

4. Double-click the graph title or graph legend.

5. In the Format Chart Title dialog box, shown in Figure 10-26, or the Format Legend dialog box, click the Patterns, Font, Alignment, or Placement (Format Legend dialog box only) tab. Make your desired edits, as shown in Figure 10-26.

6. Click OK.

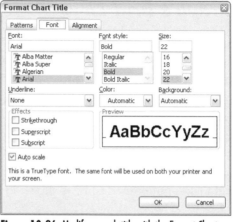

Figure 10-26: Modify a graph title with the Format Chart Title dialog box

Format a Graph's Plot Area

1. Open a presentation in PowerPoint.

2. In Normal view, under the Slides tab, select the slide that contains the graph to be modified.

3. Double-click the graph. Microsoft Graph appears, along with the graph and associated datasheet.

4. Double-click in the graph plot area.

5. In the Format Plot Area dialog box, change the border style, color, weight, or area color, as shown in Figure 10-27. Click OK to finish.

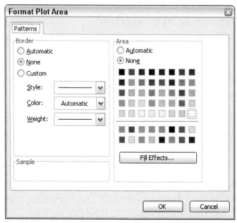

Figure 10-27: Modify a graph's plot area with the Format Plot Area dialog box

Format a Graph's Grid Lines

1. Open a presentation in PowerPoint.

2. In Normal view, under the Slides tab, select the slide that contains the graph you want to modify.

3. Double-click the graph. Microsoft Graph appears, along with the graph and associated datasheet.

4. Place the pointer near the grid line to be formatted and double-click.

5. In the Format Gridlines dialog box, click the Patterns or Scale tab and make your desired edits, as shown in Figure 10-28. Click OK.

Modify a Graph's Colors

1. Open a presentation in PowerPoint.

2. In Normal view, under the Slides tab, select the slide that contains the graph to be modified.

3. Double-click the graph. Microsoft Graph appears, along with the graph and associated datasheet.

4. Place the pointer within the graph series to be modified and double-click. Your series, which is the visual representation of your data, will be indicated by bars, columns, lines, and so on, depending on your chart type.

5. In the Format Data Series dialog box, click the Patterns tab and make your desired edits to the Series border or area, as shown in Figure 10-29. Click OK.

 With the graph series selected, you can also use the Fill Color drop-down palette in the Tables and Borders toolbar to change the series fill color.

Figure 10-28: Edit a grid line using the Format Gridlines dialog box

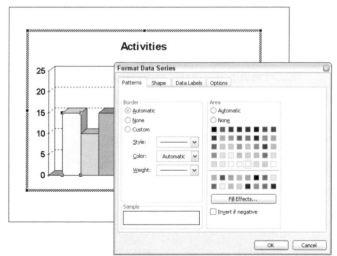

Figure 10-29: Change a graph's color in the Format Data Series dialog box

Add Labels to a Graph

1. Open a presentation in PowerPoint.

2. In Normal view, under the Slides tab, select the slide that contains the graph to be modified.

3. Double-click the graph. Microsoft Graph appears, along with the graph and associated datasheet.

4. Choose Chart➪Chart Options.

5. In the Chart Options dialog box, select the Data Labels tab.

6. Check what you would like the data label to contain, as shown in Figure 10-30. Click OK.

 Data labels can be used to further identify the data represented in a chart. The data label appears on or near the bars, columns, lines, or pie slices of your chart. Select the label text box and drag to relocate. Highlight the text and choose Format➪Font to format the label.

Modify a Graph's Axes

1. Open a presentation in PowerPoint.

2. In Normal view, under the Slides tab, select the slide that contains the graph you want to modify.

3. Double-click the graph. Microsoft Graph appears, along with the graph and associated datasheet.

4. Place the pointer on the graph axis to be modified and double-click.

5. In the Format Axis dialog box, select the Patterns, Scale, Font, Number, or Alignment tab and make your desired edits, as shown in Figure 10-31. Click OK.

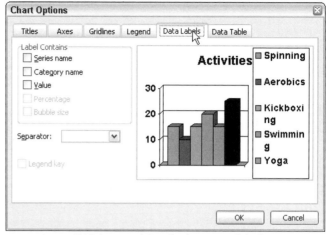

Figure 10-30: Add labels to a graph from the Chart Options dialog box

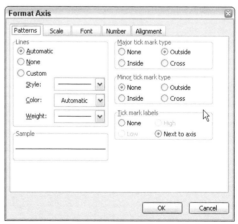

Figure 10-31: Modify a graph's axes by using the Format Axis dialog box

Creating Organizational Charts and Diagrams

Sometimes, trying to figure out who reports to whom and who is responsible for what area can be downright confusing. This is especially true for large corporations with multiple divisions, locations, and product lines. Rather than using running lists of people's names, titles, and responsibilities, it's more effective to use organizational charts. *Org charts,* as they are called in corporate circles, graphically display how a corporate hierarchy is structured. Viewers can quickly see how the company is organized — either by personnel, by function, by product, or by location. Not the corporate type? Well, organizational-type charts can also be used to display family trees, biological classifications, and other types of hierarchical information. Similarly, diagrams also offer a visual solution to presenting complicated data, especially data such as processes, workflow, relationships, and causes and effects.

Like tables and graphs, organization charts and diagrams provide important but complex and sometimes tedious information visually, making it easier and quicker for the viewer to comprehend. This chapter covers all of the tools and methods you need to create both effective and attractive org charts and diagrams.

Create a Default Organization Chart

1. Open a presentation in PowerPoint.

2. Choose Insert⇨Picture⇨Organization Chart. PowerPoint creates a chart with one top-level box and three subordinate boxes. The Organization Chart toolbar also appears, as shown in Figure 11-1.

3. Click each box (which are actually AutoShapes) and type your desired text.

4. To add additional boxes, select an existing box and click the downward-pointing arrow to the right of the Insert Shape command on the Organization Chart toolbar.

5. From the submenu, choose the relationship of the new box — Subordinate, Coworker, or Assistant. (The small icon to the left of the box type visually displays the relationship that will be created.) Briefly, choosing Subordinate adds a box below your box, choosing Coworker adds a box at the same level, and choosing Assistant adds a box between the current box and any Subordinate boxes. Note that if you want a Subordinate box, you can just click the Insert Shape button itself.

6. To delete a box, click its border and press Delete. Continue adding boxes and text as desired (see Figure 11-2).

 Lots of other organization chart templates are available from Microsoft Office Online. Choose View⇨Task Pane. Click the downward-pointing arrow and choose Select Results. Type **organization chart** in the Search field. When the results appear, select your desired template and click Download. The template will appear on your slide.

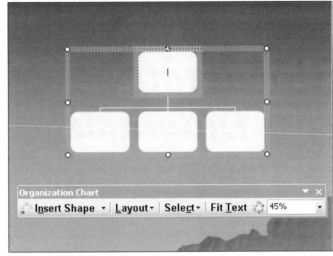

Figure 11-1: Insert an organization chart

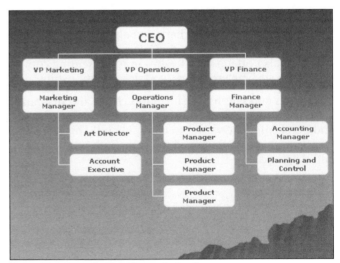

Figure 11-2: A completed simple organization chart

Modify an Organization Chart Style

1. Open a presentation in PowerPoint.

2. To modify the overall style of the organization chart, select the chart and click the AutoFormat button (lightning bolt icon) on the Organization Chart toolbar.

3. From the Organization Chart Style Gallery dialog box, choose your desired diagram style, as shown in Figure 11-3.

Modify an Organization Chart Layout

1. Open a presentation in PowerPoint.

2. To modify the overall layout of the organization chart, select the chart and click the downward-pointing arrow to the right of the Layout command on the Organization Chart toolbar.

3. From the submenu, shown in Figure 11-4, choose your desired layout type. The small icon to the left of the type visually displays the layout. Select how you want the boxes to hang from one another. Note that PowerPoint may first ask you to select a manager shape before it will change the layout. If that is the case, select one of your manager or topmost boxes and then choose your layout type.

 The AutoLayout command maintains the positions and sizes of the boxes in your organization chart. This prevents the chart from arbitrarily being changed.

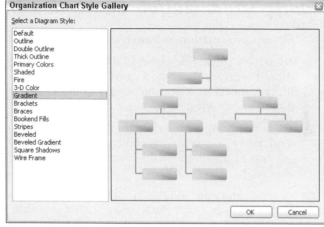

Figure 11-3: Modify an organization chart style

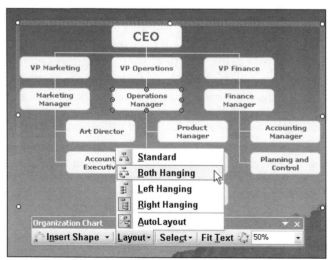

Figure 11-4: Modify an organization chart layout

Modify Organization Chart Elements

1. Open a presentation in PowerPoint.

2. To move a single box, select it, drag it by the border, and drop it onto another box. Figure 11-5 shows how we moved our Product Manager boxes to make them subordinate to a Sr. Product Manager.

3. To move multiple boxes not on the same branch or level, press the Ctrl key as you click on each box. Drag any one of the boxes by the border and drop them onto another box.

4. To move an entire level or branch of an org chart, select any box within either the level or branch you want to move. On the Organization Chart toolbar, choose Select and then either Level or Branch. Drag the manager or topmost box (all subordinates will follow) to a new location within the chart. Note that you can also select All Connecting Lines and All Assistants from the Select menu. This enables you to change the attributes of all of the connecting lines or assistant boxes (for example, stroke width or color). See Step 6.

5. To change the font, size, style, effect, or color of the text in a box, simply highlight it and choose Format⇨Font. Make your desired changes in the Font dialog box and click OK.

6. If you created a chart with the Default style, you can change the color of the fill and line of the boxes, as well as the text box attributes, by double-clicking the box. This brings up the Format AutoShape dialog box, shown in Figure 11-6. (You can also choose Format⇨AutoShape.) Choose your desired color from the Color drop-down list. You can also choose your line style, weight, and whether you want your lines dashed or solid or with (or without) arrowheads.

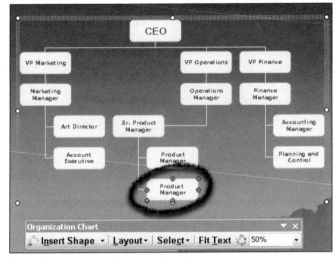

Figure 11-5: Easily move boxes around your chart

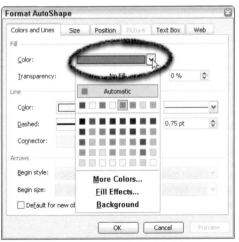

Figure 11-6: Change the color of your default boxes

Import an Organization Chart from Word or Excel

1. Open a presentation in PowerPoint.

2. Navigate to the slide on which you want to put your organization chart.

3. In either Word or Excel, select your organization chart and choose Edit➪Copy, as shown in Figure 11-7.

4. In PowerPoint, choose Edit➪Paste.

5. Your chart is inserted on the slide, as shown in Figure 11-8. You can further format or edit the org chart as desired in PowerPoint.

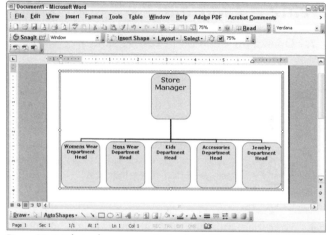

Figure 11-7: Select and copy an organization chart in Word or Excel . . .

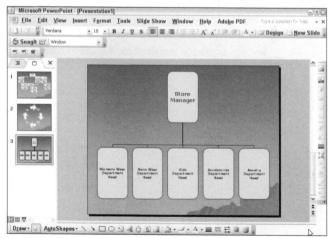

Figure 11-8: . . . and paste it into PowerPoint

Create a Diagram

1. Open a presentation in PowerPoint.

2. Choose Insert➪Diagram. You can also click the Diagram icon (three circles) in the Drawing toolbar.

3. In the Diagram Gallery dialog box, choose your desired diagram type, as shown in Figure 11-9.

 If you choose Organization Chart, it is similar to creating a default organization chart, described in the first set of steps in this chapter. To complete the chart, refer to those steps.

4. Click OK.

5. Your diagram is inserted on the slide, as shown in Figure 11-10. The Diagram toolbar also appears.

6. Click in the "Click to add text" boxes to add your desired text.

 Add emphasis to your charts and diagrams by adding animation. See how in Chapter 11.

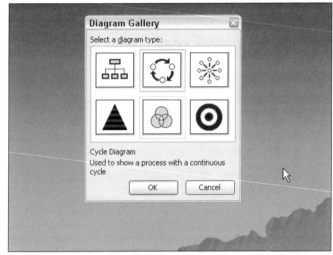

Figure 11-9: Choose your desired diagram style

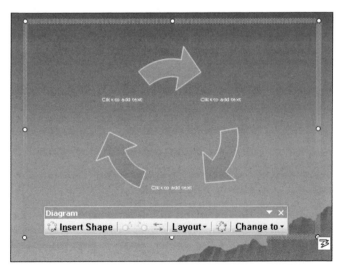

Figure 11-10: Insert a diagram into your slide

Convert a Diagram Type

1. Open a presentation in PowerPoint.

2. To convert your diagram to another type, select the diagram and click Change To in the Diagram toolbar. From the drop-down menu, choose your desired diagram style, as shown in Figure 11-11.

3. You will be presented with a warning dialog box informing you that in order to change diagram types, you must turn on AutoFormat. Click Yes.

4. We converted our diagram to a pyramid, as shown in Figure 11-12. After converting to another type, you may have to rearrange the elements in your diagram, as well as modify your text attributes.

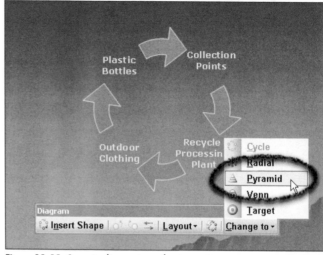

Figure 11-11: Convert a diagram to another type

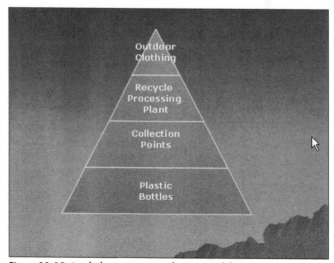

Figure 11-12: A cycle diagram is converted to a pyramid diagram

Modify a Diagram Style

1. Open a presentation in PowerPoint.

2. To modify the overall style of the diagram, select the diagram and click the AutoFormat button (lightning bolt icon) on the Diagram toolbar.

3. From the Diagram Style Gallery dialog box, choose your desired diagram style, as shown in Figure 11-13.

4. We chose the Thick Outlines style, as shown in Figure 11-14.

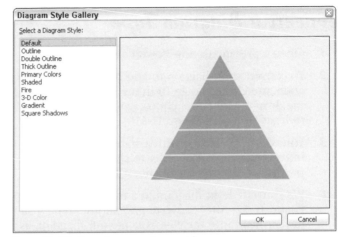

Figure 11-13: Choose from many diagram styles

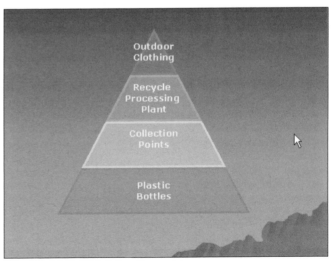

Figure 11-14: The Thick Outlines diagram style

Modify a Diagram Size

1. Open a presentation in PowerPoint.

2. To manually modify the size of the diagram, select the diagram and drag the corner sizing handle on the border. This will proportionally resize the diagram as well as the drawing space around it.

3. You can also modify the size of the diagram via the menu commands. Select the diagram and click the downward-pointing arrow to the right of the Layout command on the Diagram toolbar.

4. From the submenu, choose your desired resize method, as shown in Figure 11-15. The small icon to the left of the type visually displays the method. To make the drawing space border fit closely around the chart, choose Fit Diagram to Contents. To increase the size of the drawing area that holds the diagram but leave the diagram size unchanged, choose Expand Diagram. Resize Diagram enables you to manually size the diagram, as we did in Figure 11-16.

 The AutoLayout command maintains the positions and sizes of the boxes in your diagram. This prevents the chart from arbitrarily being changed.

Figure 11-15: Resize a diagram

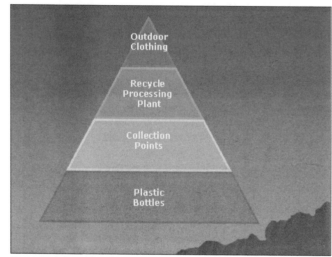

Figure 11-16: Modify a diagram

Modify Diagram Elements

1. Open a presentation in PowerPoint.

2. To add a new shape to the diagram, select it and click Insert Shape on the Diagram toolbar, as shown in Figure 11-17. To delete an existing shape, click its border and press Delete.

3. To change the font, size, style, effect, or color of the text in a diagram, select the text box and highlight the text. Then choose Format⇨Font. Make your desired changes in the Font dialog box.

4. To rearrange the text boxes in the diagram, select your desired text box and click the Move Shape Backward or Move Shape Forward (circles with curved arrows) buttons in the Diagram toolbar.

5. To reverse the entire order of your diagram, click the Reverse Diagram button (double arrow) in the Diagram toolbar.

6. If you created a diagram with the Default style, you can change the color of the fill and line of the elements by double-clicking the element. This brings up the Format AutoShape dialog box, where you can choose your desired colors (see Figure 11-18).

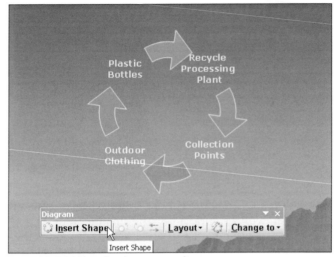

Figure 11-17: Add another element to your diagram

Figure 11-18: Change the colors of the elements in your diagram

Create a Flowchart

1. Open a presentation in PowerPoint.

2. On the Drawing toolbar, choose AutoShapes➪Flowchart. Select your desired shape from the drop-down palette, shown in Figure 11-19.

3. Drag your mouse to draw your shape.

4. Add additional shapes by repeating Step 3. If you want your shapes to be the same, simply select your first shape and choose Edit➪Copy and then Edit➪Paste as many times as you need. Select and position all of your shapes as desired, as shown in Figure 11-19.

5. Add connectors between your shapes. On the Drawing toolbar, choose AutoShapes➪Connectors. Select your desired connector style from the drop-down palette.

6. On your first shape, click where you want the beginning connector point.

7. On the next shape, click where you want the ending connector point. Note that locked connectors keep the shapes connected even if you move the shapes.

8. Repeat Steps 6 and 7 to add connectors to all of your shapes.

9. To add text to your shapes, click the shape and type text. A simple flowchart is shown in Figure 11-20.

 Note that red connector dots indicate locked connectors, while green connector dots indicate unlocked connectors. Locked connectors move with the shape. To unlock a connector, simply select the connection point and drag it away from the shape.

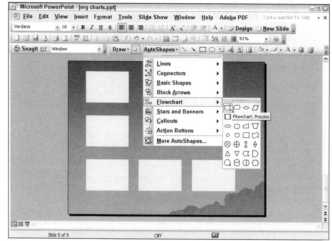

Figure 11-19: Choose your flowchart shapes

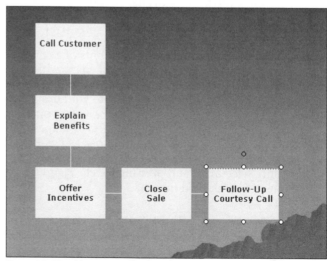

Figure 11-20: Add text to your flowchart shapes

Modify a Flowchart

1. Open a presentation in PowerPoint.

2. Select the flowchart on the slide.

3. To change the color or fill effect of a shape, select it and click the downward-pointing arrow to the right of Fill Color on the Drawing toolbar. Choose from one of the colors in the color scheme (below Automatic) or from other colors (More Fill Colors). To change the fill effect, choose Fill Effects and select from Gradient, Texture, Pattern, or Picture. For more details on these fills, see Chapter 5.

4. To change the color of a connector line, select it and click the downward-pointing arrow to the right of the Line Color button on the Drawing toolbar. To change the style of the connector line, click the Line Style button on the Drawing toolbar. You can change your solid lines to various dashed versions by clicking the Dash Style button on the Drawing toolbar, as shown in Figure 11-21.

5. To move one of the connection points of a connection line, select it and drag it to another shape within the flow chart. To move the entire connection line, select the middle of the line and drag it to your desired location. To reroute a connector to the closest point between two shapes, select one of the connected shapes and then, on the Drawing toolbar, choose Draw⇨Reroute Connectors. You can delete an unwanted connector by simply selecting it and pressing Delete. Figure 11-22 shows our modified flowchart.

 You can also double-click shapes and connector lines to bring up the Format AutoShape dialog box, where you can modify their attributes.

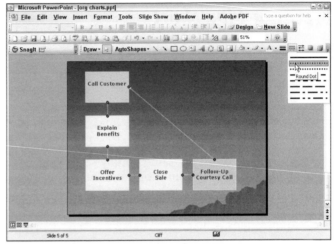

Figure 11-21: Change your connector line style

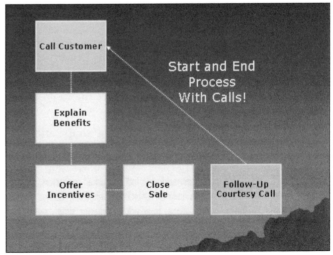

Figure 11-22: A modified flowchart

Part III
Adding a Dash of Pizzazz with Multimedia

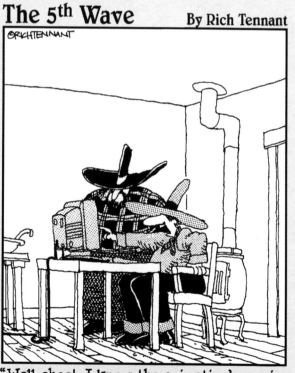

The 5th Wave   By Rich Tennant

"Well, shoot—I know the animation's moving a mite too fast, but dang if I can find a 'mosey' function in the toolbox!"

Integrating Sound and Movies

*1*f photos and illustrations add icing to your presentations, then sound and movies are the proverbial cherry on top. You can really grab the attention of your audience with the addition of audio and video elements to your presentation. What's great is that it's easy to do. A couple of menu commands are all it takes to integrate sound and movies into your slide show.

If you're short on content, PowerPoint offers quite a few media clips in its library. Music can also be imported from your own CDs or from MP3 files you have created or purchased online. Many stock photo Web sites also offer reasonably priced audio and video clips. In addition to video, you can add animated GIFs to your presentations. Animated GIFs have small file sizes and can be very effective in demonstrating a sequence.

This chapter gives you the scoop on how to integrate sound and movies into your presentations and really bring them to life.

Chapter

12

Get ready to . . .

Insert Sound from a File

1. Open a presentation in PowerPoint.

2. Go to the slide to which you want to add sound.

3. Choose Insert⇨Movies and Sound⇨Sound from File, as shown in Figure 12-1.

4. Navigate to and select the sound file you want. Then click Insert. A sound icon appears on your slide, as shown in Figure 12-2.

5. A dialog box asks whether you want the sound to play automatically when you display the slide. Click Yes or No. If you click No, the sound plays when you click the sound icon.

6. To test the sound quality, double-click the sound icon on your slide. If you are in a Slide Show view, a single click will do it.

 PowerPoint accepts the following sound file formats: WAV, WV, MP3, MPEG-4, Audio, AIF, AIFF, AIFC, MIDI, MID, KAR, MOV, MOOV, SFIL, RSRC, ALAW, AU, SND, and ULAW.

 Note that some sound file formats, like MP3 and MIDI and larger sound files, may not be embedded in your presentation but are instead linked to your presentation. So be sure to include these links with your presentation by saving it as a PowerPoint Package.

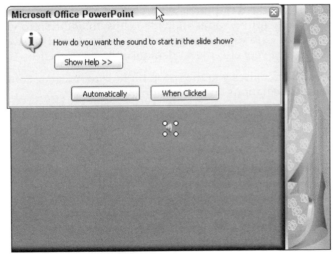

Figure 12-1: Insert a sound from a file onto your slide

Figure 12-2: Sound is indicated by an icon

Insert Sound from the Clip Organizer

1. Open a presentation in PowerPoint.

2. Go to the slide in which you want to add sound.

3. Choose Insert⇨Movies and Sound⇨Sound from Clip Organizer.

4. Select All Collections from the Show drop-down menu.

5. Choose your desired sound from the clip organizer.

6. A message box asks whether you want the sound to play automatically when you display the slide, as shown in Figure 12-3. Click Yes or No. If you click No, the sound will play when you click the sound icon. Note that if you choose to hide the sound icon, you must elect to play the sound automatically.

7. A sound icon appears on your slide, as shown in Figure 12-4.

8. To test the sound quality, double-click the sound icon on your slide. To remove the sound, simply select and delete the icon.

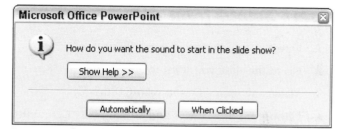

Figure 12-3: Choose whether to play the sound automatically or manually

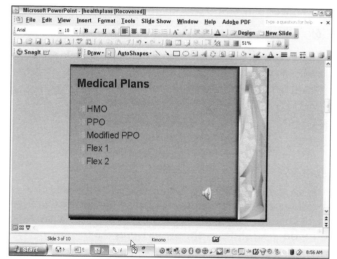

Figure 12-4: Sounds are indicated on the slide by a speaker icon

Insert Sound from a CD

1. Open a presentation in PowerPoint.

2. Go to the slide you want to add sound to.

3. Make sure your CD is in your CD drive.

4. Choose Insert➪Movies and Sound➪Play CD Audio Track.

5. In the Insert CD Audio dialog box, select your desired track (song) or tracks, as shown in Figure 12-5.

6. Set your Timing, Play, and Display options:

   - Check Loop Until Stopped to have your music repeatedly play until you stop it.

   - Click the Sound Volume icon to access the volume slider.

   - Finally, you can choose to hide the sound icon during your slide show.

7. Click OK.

8. A dialog box asks whether you want the sound to play automatically when you display the slide or when you click the CD icon. Click your choice. A CD icon appears on your slide, as shown in Figure 12-6.

9. To test the sound quality, double-click the CD icon on your slide.

 Remember, the music from the CD will not be embedded into your presentation. You must have the actual CD in your CD drive to play the music during your show.

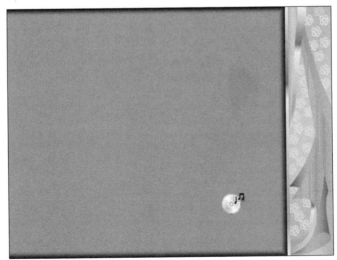

Figure 12-5: Insert an audio track from a CD

Figure 12-6: A CD icon indicates audio from a CD

Record a Comment

1. Open a presentation in PowerPoint.

2. Go to the slide to which you want to add your comment. (Comments are meant to be recorded on a single slide. To record a voice throughout the presentation, see "Record a Narration.")

3. Choose Insert⇨Movies and Sound⇨Record Sound.

 In order to record a comment or a narration, make sure your computer is outfitted with a sound card, a microphone, and speakers.

4. In the Record Sound dialog box, name your comment, as shown in Figure 12-7.

5. In the Record Sound dialog box, click the Record button (the red circle) and speak into the microphone.

6. When you are done with your comment, click the Stop button (the blue square).

7. To play the comment back, click the Play button (the blue triangle).

8. Repeat Steps 2 through 6 for any other slides you want to add comments to.

9. Click OK. A sound icon appears on the slide.

 If the quality of the sound is vital, it may be worth looking into free recording programs, like Audacity, which provide more controls and produce a superior-quality sound over the Windows recorder.

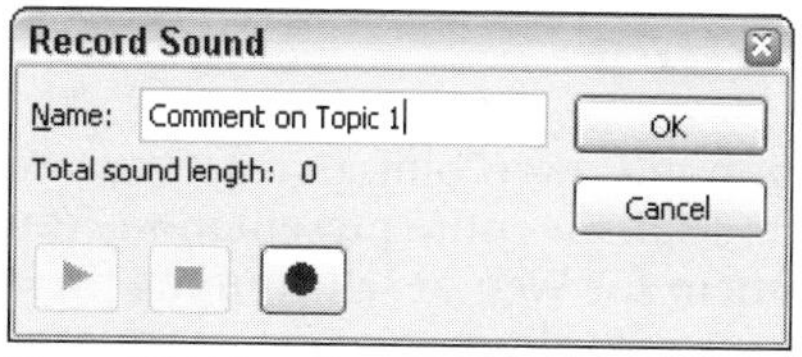

Record Sound

Name: Comment on Topic 1

Total sound length: 0

OK

Cancel

Figure 12-7: Record a comment in your presentation

Record a Narration

1. Open a presentation in PowerPoint. (Narrations are designed to run through an entire presentation. You may want to use them for Web or self-running presentations. For short voice recordings on a single slide, see "Record a Comment.")

2. In Normal view, in the Slide tab area, select the slide you want to start your narration on.

3. Choose Slide Show⇨Record Narration.

4. In the Record Narration dialog box, shown in Figure 12-8, perform the following actions:

   - Click the Set Microphone Level button to specify your desired volume. Click OK.

   - Adjust the quality by clicking the Change Quality button. In the Sound Selection dialog box, shown in Figure 12-9, choose from CD Quality (highest) to Telephone Quality (lowest) from the Name dropdown list and then click OK. Note that the higher the sound quality, the larger the file size.

5. Choose whether or not to link your narration to your presentation. If you choose to link your narration, click the Browse button and select the folder in which you want to save your narration file. If you do not link your narration, it will be embedded into your presentation. It is recommended that larger narrations be linked. This enables your presentation file to remain at a manageable size. Remember to include the linked narration file with your presentation file on your hard drive or on any external media.

6. Click OK to exit the Record Narration dialog box.

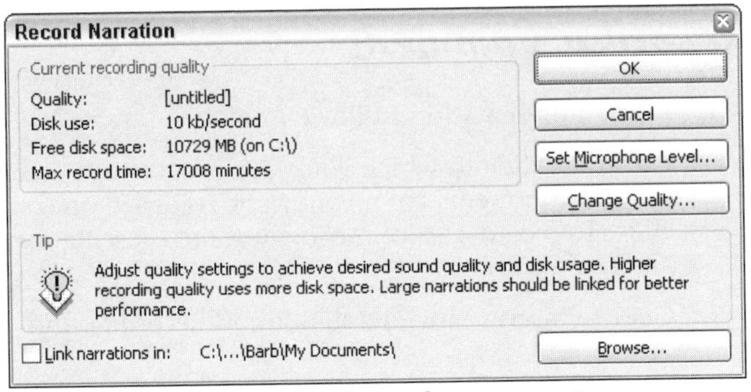

Figure 12-8: Record a voiceover, or narration, for your presentation

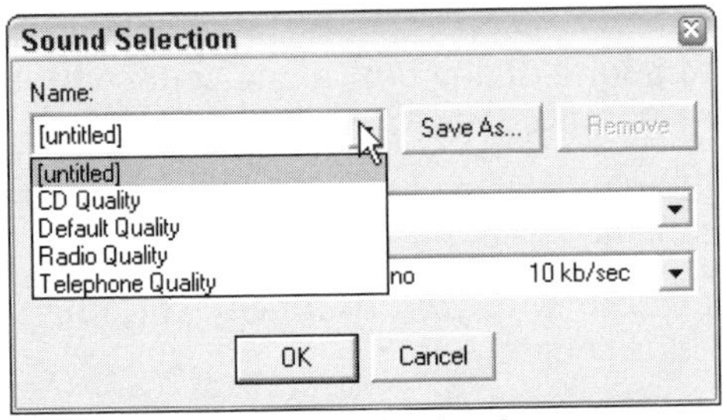

Figure 12-9: Specify the sound quality of your narration

 Note that PowerPoint can play only one sound file at a time. Therefore, if you have other sounds that play automatically in your presentation, the narration overrides those sounds.

7. If you chose the first slide in your presentation in Step 2, proceed to Step 8. If you selected another slide in your presentation in Step 2, a second, smaller Record Narration dialog box appears. Click either Current Slide or First Slide to indicate where you want your narration to begin.

8. Your presentation will now appear in Slide Show view, as shown in Figure 12-10. Speak your narration into the microphone. When you are done with the narration for that slide, click the slide to advance to the next slide. Continue your narration for the next slide. Repeat these steps for your entire presentation.

 You can pause your narration by right-clicking the slide and choosing Pause Narration from the context menu. To resume your narration, choose Resume Narration using the same method.

 If you make a mistake, you can re-record part of the narration. Go to the slide you want to re-record and follow Steps 1 through 7. When you are done re-recording the portions you want to change, press Esc and go to Step 10.

9. When the black "end of presentation" screen appears, click it.

10. Your narration is saved. A message appears, asking you whether you would also like to save the slide timings (shown below each slide). If you click Save, your presentation will appear in Slide Sorter view with timings displayed under each slide, as shown in Figure 12-11. If you click Don't Save, you will return to your first slide.

 You can run your slide show without the narration or with the narration but without your saved timings (choose Manually under Advance slides) by selecting those commands under Slide Show➪ Set Up Show.

Figure 12-10: Add narration to your presentation in Slide Show view

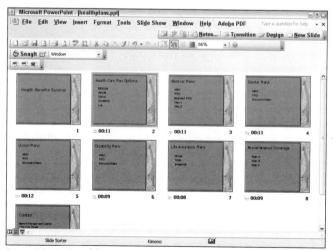

Figure 12-11: Your slide timings for your narration appear under each slide

Insert an Animated GIF from a File

1. Open a presentation in PowerPoint.

2. Go to the slide to which you want to add your animated GIF.

3. Choose Insert⇨Movies and Sounds⇨Movie from File.

4. Navigate to and select your animated GIF file and click Insert.

5. A dialog box asks whether you want the GIF to play automatically when you display the slide. Click Yes or No. If you click No, the GIF will play when you click the GIF frame. The first frame of the animated GIF appears on your slide, as shown in Figure 12-12.

6. To preview the animated GIF, right-click the GIF and click Play in the Custom Animation task pane.

Insert a Movie from a File

1. Open a presentation in PowerPoint.

2. Go to the slide to which you want to add a movie.

3. Choose Insert⇨Movies and Sounds⇨Movie from File, as shown in Figure 12-13.

4. Navigate to and select your movie file and click Insert. The first frame of the movie appears on your slide.

5. A dialog box asks whether you want the movie to play automatically when you display the slide. Click Yes or No. If you click No, the movie will play when you click the movie frame.

6. To preview the movie, double-click the frame on your slide.

PowerPoint accepts the following movie file formats: AVI, DVR-MS, MP2V, MP3, M3U, MPA, M1V, MPE, MPEG, MPG, .ASF, WP2, WPL, WM, WMD, WMV, WMX.

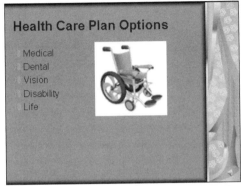

Figure 12-12: Insert an animated GIF into your presentation

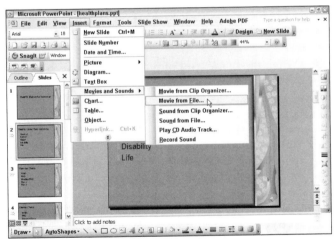

Figure 12-13: Insert a movie clip into your presentation

Insert an Animated GIF or Movie from the Clip Organizer

1. Open a presentation in PowerPoint.

2. Go to the slide to which you want to add a movie.

3. Choose Insert➪Movies and Sounds➪Movie from Clip Organizer.

4. The Clip Art task pane appears, as shown in Figure 12-14. If you know where your GIF or movie clip is located, scroll through the library and select it. If you're unsure, you can enter the name or keyword of your desired file in the Search For field. You can restrict your search to just Movies or Animated GIFs by checking your desired media types and file formats in the Selected Media File Types drop-down list. Click Go. Locate and then click your desired file in the library.

5. A dialog box asks whether you want the movie or GIF to play automatically when you display the slide. Click Yes or No. If you click No, the movie or GIF will play when you click the movie frame. The first frame of the movie appears on your slide, as shown in Figure 12-15.

6. To preview the movie, double-click the frame on your slide. To preview the animated GIF, right-click the GIF and click Play in the Custom Animation task pane.

 You can preview any clip by positioning your mouse cursor over the thumbnail in the Clip Art task pane library and clicking the downward-pointing arrow. Select Preview/Properties from the drop-down list. Click the arrow in the Preview/Properties dialog box to play the clip.

Figure 12-14: Insert a movie clip from the Clip Organizer

Figure 12-15: The first frame of your movie appears on the slide

Resize a Movie

1. Open a presentation in PowerPoint.

2. Go to the slide that contains your movie clip.

3. Select the clip and do one of the following:

   - Right-click and select Edit Movie Object. Check Zoom to Full Screen to have the movie play on the full screen during the slide show.

   - Position your mouse cursor over one of the corner sizing handles. Drag the movie frame larger or smaller, as shown in Figure 12-16. Press the Ctrl key to keep the center of the movie in the same location.

   - Choose Format⇨Picture. Click the Size tab (see Figure 12-17). Enter your desired dimensions in the Width and Height boxes or choose a scaling percentage. Select Lock Aspect Ratio to keep the movie in proportion. You can also choose Best Scale for Slide Show. This option ensures that the movie is optimized for the best display and playback.

4. Click OK.

Figure 12-16: Resize your movie manually

Figure 12-17: Resize your movie with the Size dialog box

Edit Movie and Sound Options

1. Open a presentation in PowerPoint.

2. Go to the slide that contains your sound or movie clip.

3. Select the clip and right-click it.

4. Select Edit Movie Object or Edit Sound Object from the context menu.

5. Specify your settings in the Movie Options or Sound Options dialog box (see Figure 12-18):

   - **Loop until stopped:** The movie or sound will play repeatedly until you stop it.

   - **Rewind movie when done playing:** The movie will automatically rewind to the first frame after playing once.

   - **Sound volume:** Click the icon to access the volume slider.

   - **Hide while not playing:** Icons and frames will be hidden when they aren't playing.

   - **Zoom to full screen:** The movie will play full-screen, as shown in Figure 12-19. When it is done, the slide will return on-screen.

6. Click OK.

 You can use the Custom Animation task pane to play, pause, and stop a movie. You can also use this task pane to further animate a sound or movie object. For example, you can have the first frame of your movie or your sound icon move into the frame and begin playing. See Chapter 11 for further details on animation.

Figure 12-18: Edit your movie and sound options

Figure 12-19: A movie in full-screen mode

Incorporate Hyperlinks and Transitions

You might think a basic office program such as PowerPoint is incapable of adding any snap, crackle, and pop to your presentations. Think again. Underneath PowerPoint's conservative attire lies a whole bevy of special effects that you can apply to your slides. If you need to jump to a Web site or to another file or presentation during your slide show, you simply insert a hyperlink. Advancing from one slide to the next can be elegant and unobtrusive with slow fades, or dynamic and active with wipes and spins. With this chapter's help, your presentations will be snapping, crackling, and popping to their heart's content!

Chapter

13

Get ready to . . .

Create a Hyperlink in a Presentation

1. Open a presentation in PowerPoint.

2. Go to the slide that contains the element you want to use as your source link in the hyperlink.

3. Choose the element (we chose a small circular autoshape) and then choose Insert⇨Hyperlink or click the Hyperlink button on the Standard toolbar, as shown in Figure 13-1.

4. In the Insert Hyperlink dialog box, select the Place in This Document option under Link To, as shown in Figure 13-2.

5. Select your desired destination link under Select a Place in This Document. Select from the slides or a custom show within your presentation. If you select a custom show, you can mark the Show and Return check box, which will take the display back to the source link after the show has played. For more on custom shows, see Chapter 16.

6. Click OK.

7. To test your hyperlink, run your presentation by choosing Slide Show⇨View Show. You can also click the Slide Show from Current Slide button at the bottom of the Slides tab in Normal view. Note that when you hover your cursor over the hyperlink, the arrow becomes a pointing hand, indicating a link.

 Hyperlinks are links from one slide to another slide, a custom show (a sub presentation within your main presentation), a Web site, an e-mail address, or a file. The hyperlink can be text, a picture, an AutoShape, a chart, WordArt, or an action button. (We describe action buttons later in this chapter.)

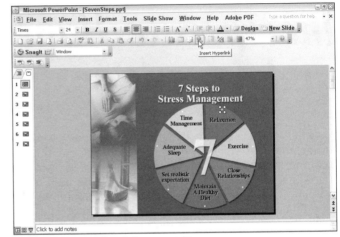

Figure 13-1: Assign a hyperlink to text or objects

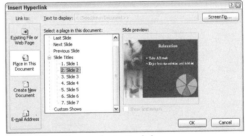

Figure 13-2: Choose a destination link
Photo Credit: Corbis Images, PhotoDisc/Getty Images

Insert a Hyperlink to a File or Web Site

1. Open a presentation in PowerPoint.

2. Go to the slide that contains the element you want to use as your source link in the hyperlink.

3. Choose the element (we chose a small circular AutoShape) and then choose Insert⇨Hyperlink or click the Hyperlink button on the Standard toolbar.

4. In the Insert Hyperlink dialog box, click Existing File or Web Page under Link To, as shown in Figure 13-3.

5. Navigate to your desired file or type your Web site URL in the Address field.

6. Click OK.

Note that a hyperlink is automatically created when you type a Web site URL on a slide in your presentation outline. Note that the link is active in Slide Show view only.

To cancel the display of a hyperlinked Web page, choose View⇨ Toolbars⇨Web. Click the Stop button (page icon with an X) in the Web toolbar.

Figure 13-3: Create a hyperlink to a file or Web site

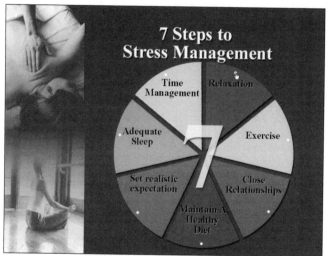

Figure 13-4: Hyperlinks are indicated by a pointing figure icon

Insert a Hyperlink to a New File

1. Open a presentation in PowerPoint.

2. Go to the slide that contains the element you want to use as your source link in the hyperlink.

3. Choose the element (we chose a small circular AutoShape) and then choose Insert⇨Hyperlink or click the Hyperlink button on the Standard toolbar.

4. In the Insert Hyperlink dialog box, click Create New Document under Link To.

5. Type the name of your new document, as shown in Figure 13-5.

6. Click the Change button to navigate to the location where you would like to save the new documents. Note that the path to that location will be recorded.

7. In the Create New Document dialog box, shown in Figure 13-6, select the type of file format you want for your new document. For ours, we selected a .doc file format.

8. Choose whether to edit the new document now or later. If you choose now, the program to create your new document will be launched. You can then enter any text you want to appear when the document is opened. If you choose later, the program will be launched and a new document will be created when the user first clicks the hyperlink during the slide show. The program that is launched depends on the file format you chose in Step 7. When we click our hyperlink, Word launches because our file format is a .doc file.

9. Click OK.

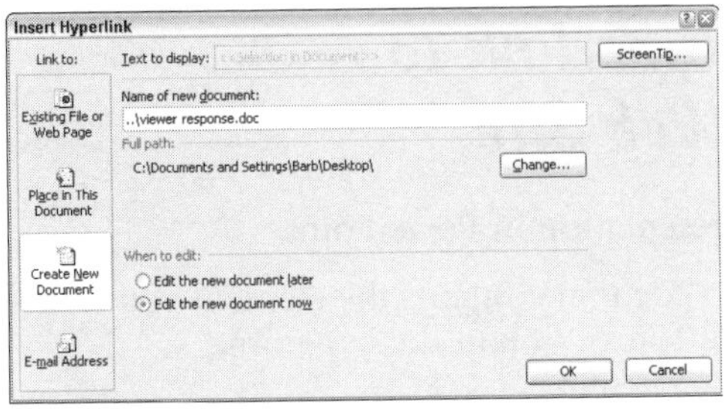

Figure 13-5: Create a hyperlink to a new file

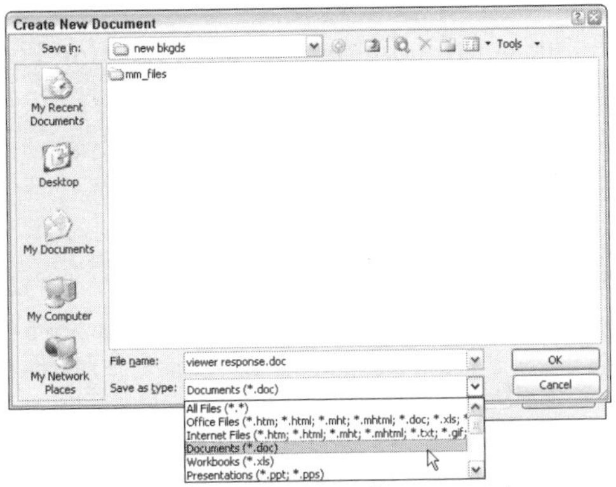

Figure 13-6: Select the right format for your new document

Insert a Hyperlink to an E-Mail Address

1. Open a presentation in PowerPoint.

2. Go to the slide that contains the element you want to use as your source link in the hyperlink.

3. Choose the element (we chose a small circular AutoShape) and then choose Insert⇨Hyperlink or click the Hyperlink button on the Standard toolbar.

4. In the Insert Hyperlink dialog box, select E-Mail Address under Link To, shown in Figure 13-7.

5. Type your desired e-mail address. You can also select an e-mail address in the Recently Used E-Mail Addresses box.

6. Type the subject you want to appear in the e-mail subject line.

7. Click OK.

8. When the hyperlink is clicked in the slide show, the default e-mail client will launch and a new message window will open, as shown in Figure 13-8.

 Note that a hyperlink is automatically created when you type an e-mail address on a slide in your presentation outline. Note that the link is active in Slide Show view only.

Figure 13-7: Create a hyperlink to an e-mail address

Figure 13-8: The default e-mail client is launched when you click the hyperlink
Photo Credit: Corbis Images, PhotoDisc/Getty Images

Insert a Hyperlink to Another Presentation

1. Open a presentation in PowerPoint.

2. Go to the slide that contains the element you want to use as your source link in the hyperlink.

3. Choose the element (we chose a small circular AutoShape) and then choose Insert⇨Hyperlink or click the Hyperlink button on the Standard toolbar.

4. In the Insert Hyperlink dialog box, click Existing File or Web Page under Link To.

5. Navigate to and select the presentation that contains the slide you want to designate as your destination link.

6. Click the Bookmark button in the top-right corner. In the Select Place in Document dialog box, shown in Figure 13-9, select the slide you want to link to.

7. Click OK and OK again to exit the dialog box and apply the hyperlink.

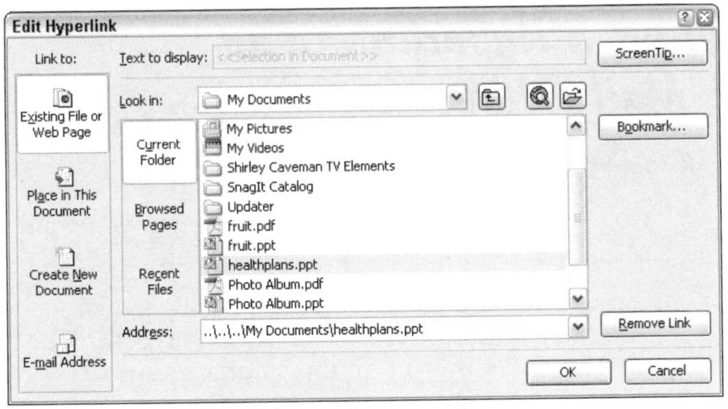

Figure 13-9: Create a hyperlink to another presentation

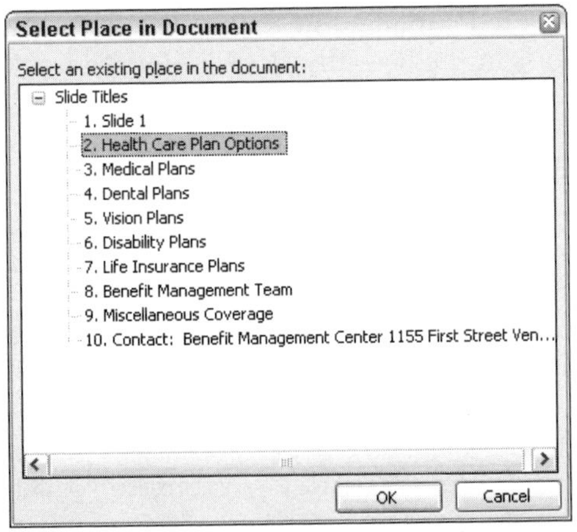

Figure 13-10: Choose your desired slide within the presentation

Change the Color of Hyperlinked Text

1. Open a presentation in PowerPoint.

2. Select Format⇨Slide Design.

3. In the Slide Design task pane, click Color Schemes.

4. In the Edit Color Scheme dialog box, shown in Figure 13-11, select the Accent and Hyperlink check box or Accent and Followed Hyperlink check box and click Change Color.

5. Select a color from either the Standard or Custom color palettes and click OK. For more on Standard and Custom colors, see Chapter 8.

6. Click Apply.

7. The colors of your hyperlinked text before you click them and after they have been clicked will be changed, as shown in Figure 13-12.

The color of your hyperlinks will also change when you choose a different color scheme. To change your color scheme, select your desired slides in the Slides tab. Choose Format⇨Slide Design. Click Color Schemes at the top of the pane. Then choose your desired color scheme from the list.

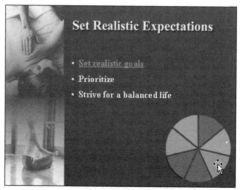

Figure 13-11: Assign a different color to your hyperlinked text

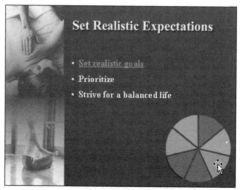

Figure 13-12: Hyperlinked text now appears pink
Photo Credit: Corbis Images, PhotoDisc/Getty Images

Show Highlights or Play Sounds on Hyperlinks

1. Open a presentation in PowerPoint.

2. Select the hyperlinked text or object.

3. Choose Slide Show⇨Action Settings.

4. In the Action Settings dialog box, shown in Figure 13-13, select one of the following:

   - **Mouse Click:** This option applies the action when the mouse is clicked on the hyperlink object.

   - **Mouse Over:** This applies the action when the mouse is pointed on the hyperlink object.

5. Assign the action to the hyperlink:

   - **Hyperlink To:** If you already have a destination link established, you can ignore this setting. If you select a custom show, type the name of the show. If you select a URL, type the location of the Web site. If you select another PowerPoint presentation or file, navigate to the location on your hard drive and select the file.

   - **Play Sound:** Select this check box to have your hyperlink object play a sound when you click or point to it. Select your desired sound from the drop-down list. Select a PowerPoint preset sound or your own sound file. Note that the sound must be in the .wav file format.

   - **Highlight Click:** Select this check box to have your hyperlink object highlighted when you click or point to it, as shown in Figure 13-14.

6. Click OK.

Figure 13-13: Assign sounds or highlighting to your hyperlink object

Figure 13-14: Highlight your hyperlink object by clicking or pointing with your mouse
Photo Credit: PhotoSpin

Insert an Action Button

1. Open a presentation in PowerPoint.

2. Go to the slide on which you want to insert an action button.

3. Choose Slide Show↪Action Buttons.

4. Choose your desired button from the submenu, as shown in Figure 13-15.

5. Click on the slide to place the button.

6. In the Action Settings dialog box, specify your desired action. Select Mouse Click or Mouse Over by clicking the desired tab. Then set the destination link for your hyperlink. You can also assign a sound to the action. For details on these settings, see the preceding section, "Show Highlights or Play Sounds on Hyperlinks."

7. Click OK.

8. On our slide, shown in Figure 13-16, we chose Previous and Next buttons. When the user clicks, he will be taken to the previous or next slide. We also shrank our buttons by simply dragging a corner sizing handle.

 Insert action buttons (such as Previous, Next, and Play) to help your viewers navigate through your presentation. This is especially helpful for self-running presentations on the Web or in kiosks.

 You can also insert action buttons on all your slides. Simply insert the action buttons on your slide master(s). For more on slide masters, see Chapter 4.

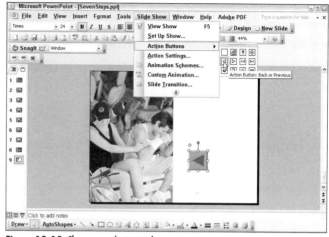

Figure 13-15: Choose your button style

Figure 13-16: Arrange and size your actions buttons
Photo Credit: PhotoSpin

Add a Transition to All Slides

1. Open a presentation in PowerPoint.

2. Select Slide Show⇨Slide Transition.

3. In the Slide Transition task pane, shown in Figure 13-17, select your desired transition.

4. Click Apply to All Slides.

5. Specify the speed of your transitions. Select Slow, Medium, or Fast.

6. You can also attach a sound to your transition. Select one of the presets from the PowerPoint library or select Other Sound from the drop-down list to navigate to your own sound file.

7. Choose whether to automatically advance to the next slide after a specified number of seconds or to advance by clicking your mouse.

8. To preview the transition, shown in Figure 13-18, click the Play button. To play the slide show from your current slide forward, click Slide Show.

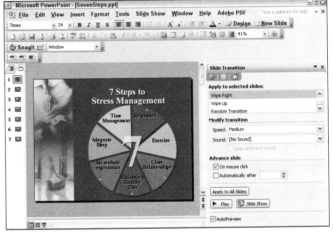

Figure 13-17: Apply transitions to your slides

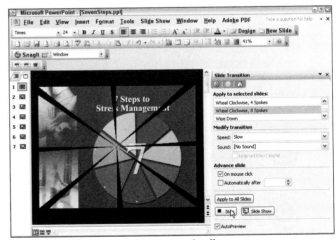

Figure 13-18: Play your transition to preview the effect

Add a Different Transition to Each Slide

1. Open a presentation in PowerPoint.

2. In Normal view, under the Slides tab, select your desired slides for the first transition.

3. Select Slide Show⇨Slide Transition.

4. In the Slide Transition task pane, select your desired transition.

5. Repeat Steps 2 through 4 for all the slides in your presentation.

6. For specifying transition settings, see the earlier section, "Add a Transition to All Slides."

 Transitions are effects used to advance from one slide to the next. Although transitions are fun, be careful about using too many different kinds of transitions. You want your audience to pay attention to your content, not be distracted by your special effects, or worse, get motion sickness.

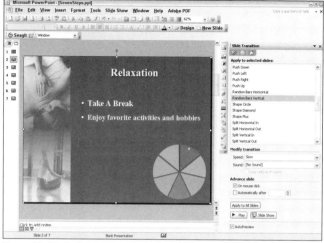

Figure 13-19: Apply transitions to individual slides

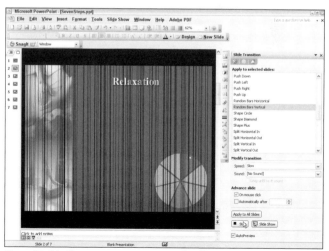

Figure 13-20: Play your transition to preview the effect

Incorporate Animation

*I*f the previous chapter on hyperlinks and transitions didn't add enough pizzazz to your presentations, you may want to step it up a bit and employ custom animations to the elements on your slides. You can easily have your text fly in from the left and then dim or change color after it has played. Or you can create a custom motion path and have your object follow a map on your slide. If motion isn't enough, you can easily attach sounds, such as camera clicks or voltage zaps, to your animations.

This chapter shows you how to employ animation for added emphasis and impact in your presentations.

Chapter

14

Get ready to . . .

Apply Animation Schemes

1. Open a presentation in PowerPoint.

2. In Normal view, under the Slides tab, select your desired slide(s) for the animation.

3. Choose Slide Show⇨Animation Schemes.

4. In the Slide Design task pane, select your desired animation scheme from the Apply to Selected Slides list, as shown in Figure 14-1. This applies the animation to your selected slide. Deselect AutoPreview to prevent automatically seeing the animation when you select it from the list.

5. Click Apply to All Slides if you want to apply the animation scheme to all slides in your presentation.

6. Click Play to preview the effect on your displayed slide.

7. Click Slide Show to play the presentation from your displayed slide forward.

8. To delete an animation scheme, select No Animation from the Apply to Selected Slides list.

 Animation schemes are applied to the entire slide. To animate text or individual objects, see the next section.

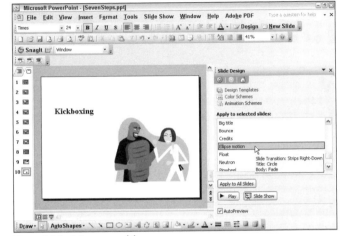

Figure 14-1: Animate your slides

Create a Motion Path for Animations

1. Open a presentation in PowerPoint.

2. In Normal view, under the Slides tab, select the slide that contains the object for which you want to create a motion path.

3. Select the object on the slide.

4. Choose Slide Show⇨Custom Animation.

5. In the Custom Animation task pane, click Add Effect and then select Motion Paths, as shown in Figure 14-2.

6. Choose from the following:

   - **Preset Motion Path:** Choose from one of the preset paths.

   - **Draw Custom Path:** Choose from one of four ways to draw your path. *Freeform* enables you to draw a path with curved (drag) and straight (click and move mouse) lines. *Scribble* enables you to drag curved lines as if you were using a pen on paper, as shown in Figure 14-3. *Line* lets you drag straight lines. And *Curve* lets you draw by clicking where you want your curves.

   - **More Motion Paths:** Choose from additional preset paths.

7. Your motion path appears on the slide.

8. Click Play to preview the effect on your displayed slide.

9. Click Slide Show to play the presentation from your displayed slide forward.

Figure 14-2: Apply a motion path to your animated object

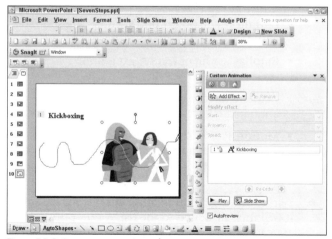

Figure 14-3: Draw a custom motion path

Apply a Custom Animation to Text or Objects

1. Open a presentation in PowerPoint.

2. In Normal view, under the Slides tab, select the slide that contains the text or object you want to animate.

3. Select the text or object on the slide. If you select the text box placeholder, all the text within the box will animate. Highlight individual sections of text within the box to have them animate individually.

4. Choose Slide Show⇨Custom Animation.

5. In the Custom Animation task pane, shown in Figure 14-4, select how you would like your text or object to appear on the slide by clicking Add Effect and selecting from the following:

   • **Entrance:** The object or text enters the slide show with the animated effect.

   • **Emphasis:** The object or text is animated while it is on the slide.

   • **Exit:** The object or text leaves the slide show with the animated effect.

   • **Motion Paths:** The object or text moves by following a specific path and direction. For details, see the preceding section, "Create a Motion Path for Animations."

6. Select your desired animation effect from the submenu. It will then be added to the list. A non-printing number appears next to your text or object, and this number corresponds to the animation effect in the list. The number also does not appear in the slide show.

Figure 14-4: Add animation to individual objects and text

Figure 14-5: Specify the direction and speed of your animation effect

7. Specify your animation settings. Choose how you want your animation to start. Also specify the direction and speed of the animation movement, as shown in Figure 14-5.

8. Click Play to preview the effect on your displayed slide, as shown in Figures 14-6 and 14-7. Note the timeline that appears when you play your effects to demonstrate your timing.

9. Click Slide Show to play the presentation from your displayed slide forward.

10. To edit an animation, select the effect from the list and click Change. Then follow Steps 5 through 7 in this list.

11. To delete an animation effect, select it and click Remove.

 You can apply animations to text, objects, and even diagrams and charts. Objects can consist of AutoShapes, clip art, photos, sounds, and movies.

 You can animate individual elements of a chart by selecting them in your chart and applying an effect. Then click the down-pointing arrow to the right of the effect and, from the context menu, choose Effect options. Click the Chart Animation or Diagram Animation tab. From the Group Chart or Group Diagram drop-down list, select an option, such as Each Branch or Up or Down. Options will depend on the type of chart or diagram.

 Animations are listed in the order you apply them. You can rearrange the order by selecting the effect and clicking the Re-Order arrows.

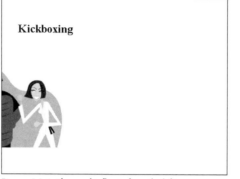

Figure 14-6: The graphic flies in from the left . . .

Figure 14-7: . . . and ends up on the right

Apply Animation to Bullets

1. Open a presentation in PowerPoint.

2. In Normal view, under the Slides tab, select the slide that contains the bulleted text you want to animate.

3. Choose Slide Show⇨Custom Animation.

4. Select the first bulleted text.

5. In the Custom Animation task pane, shown in Figure 14-8, choose how you would like your bulleted text to appear on the slide by clicking Add Effect and then choosing Entrance.

6. From the Entrance submenu, choose your desired animation effect.

7. Leave your Start option set to On Click.

8. Specify your desired speed for the bullet.

9. Click Play to preview the effect on your displayed slide.

10. Click Slide Show to play the presentation from your displayed slide forward.

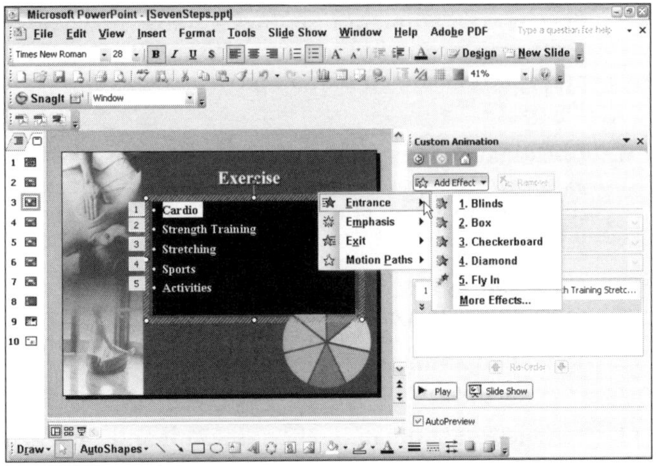

Figure 14-8: Animate your bulleted text for more emphasis
Photo Credit: Corbis Images, PhotoDisc/Getty Images

Apply Additional Effects to Animated Bullets

1. Open a presentation in PowerPoint.

2. In Normal view, under the Slides tab, select the slide that contains the animation effect you want to enhance.

3. Choose Slide Show⇨Custom Animation.

4. In the Custom Animation task pane, select your animated effect from the list and then click the down-pointing arrow to the right. You can also select all the effects and click the arrow for the last one in the list.

5. From the context menu, choose Effect Options, as shown in Figure 14-9.

6. In the dialog box for your specific animation effect (ours happens to be Fade), under the Effect tab, select the desired enhancements. For the Fade effect, your choices are as follows:

   • **Sound:** Select a sound effect to attach to your animation. If you select Other Sound, navigate to your desired sound on your hard drive.

   • **After animation:** Choose whether to dim or hide your text after the animation or after your next mouse click, as shown in Figure 14-10. You can also have your text or object change colors after the animation.

   • **Animate text:** Choose whether to have your bulleted text animate all at once or by each word or letter. If you choose by word or letter, specify the percentage of delay between words or letters.

7. Click OK.

8. Click Play to preview the effect on your displayed slide.

9. Click Slide Show to play the presentation from your displayed slide forward.

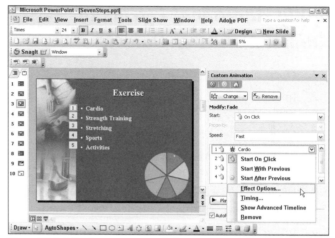

Figure 14-9: Add enhancements to your bullets

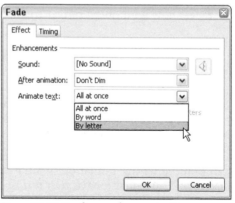

Figure 14-10: Specify your enhancement settings
Photo Credit: Corbis Images, PhotoDisc/Getty Images

Apply Additional Effects to Animated Text or Objects

1. Open a presentation in PowerPoint.

2. In Normal view, under the Slides tab, select the slide that contains the animation effect you want to enhance.

3. Choose Slide Show⇨Custom Animation.

4. In the Custom Animation task pane, select your animated effect from the list.

5. Click the down-pointing arrow to the right and then choose Effect Options from the context menu.

6. In the dialog box for your specific animation effect (ours is Fly In), under the Effect tab, select the desired enhancements. For Fly In, your choices are as follows:

    -   **Direction:** Select how your object or text enters the slide.

    -   **Smooth Start/Smooth End:** Select these check boxes, shown in Figure 14-11, to smooth out the movement of the animation as it enters or leaves the slide.

    -   **Sound:** Select a sound effect to attach to your animation. If you select Other Sound, navigate to your desired sound on your hard drive.

    -   **After Animation:** Choose whether to dim or hide your text or object after the animation or after your next mouse click. You can also have your text or object change colors after the animation.

    -   **Animate Text:** Choose whether to have your text animate all at once or by each word or letter. If you choose by word or letter, specify the percentage of delay between words or letters.

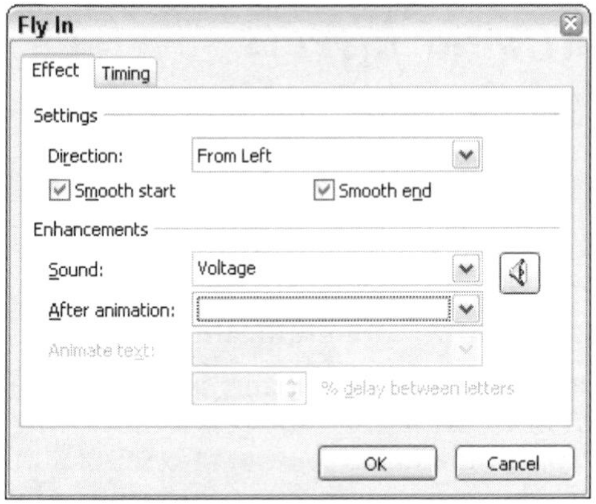

Figure 14-11: Add enhancements to your animations

Figure 14-12: Specify your animation timing options

7. In the dialog box for your specific animation effect, on the Timing tab, select the specific enhancements you want. For Fly In, your choices are as follows:

   - **Start:** Specify how you want the animation to begin, as shown in Figure 14-12. Choose from on mouse click, along with the previous animation, or after the previous animation plays through.

   - **Delay:** Specify whether you want a delay between the end of one animation and the beginning of the next.

   - **Speed:** Choose from a variety of speeds for your animation.

   - **Repeat:** Choose how many times you want the animation to *loop* (repeat).

   - **Rewind When Done Playing:** If you select this check box, the animation will automatically rewind when it's done playing and return to its original state/position on the slide.

   - **Triggers:** Specify whether the animation plays when the mouse is just clicked or when the mouse is clicked on a specific object or piece of text.

8. Click OK.

9. Click Play to preview the effect on your displayed slide. (See Figures 14-13 and 14-14.)

10. Click Slide Show to play the presentation from your displayed slide forward.

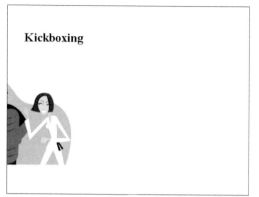

Kickboxing

Figure 14-13: The graphics flies in smoothly to a voltage sound effect . . .

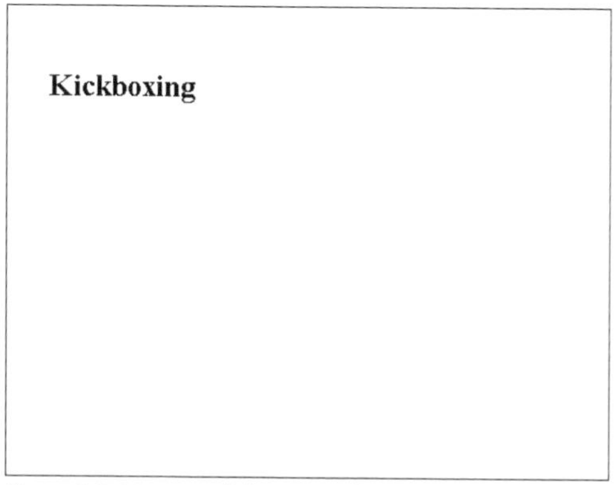

Kickboxing

Figure 14-14: . . . and changes to white

Part IV
Presenting Effectively

Preparing the Presentation

After you've done all the hard work of compiling and formatting the content of your presentation, it's time to get it ready to share with the world. Begin by specifying the display options for your show. Determine how your show will be presented. Will a speaker control it, or will it be self-running on a kiosk? Choose whether your show will loop continuously and whether it will include narration and animation. Establish your timings and optimize your display performance.

When your show is ready to go, print your outline and all your notes and handouts. And last but not least, be sure to make a backup of your hard-earned presentation by packaging it to a CD. You want to be prepared if your original presentation stored on the computer's hard drive goes awry.

Get ready to . . .

Set Up Your Show

1. Open a presentation in PowerPoint.

2. Choose Slide Show⊏⇒Set Up Show.

3. In the Set Up Show dialog box, shown in Figure 15-1, specify the following settings:

   - **Show Type:** The Presented by a Speaker option displays a full-screen slide show that is controlled by a speaker. The Browsed by an Individual option displays in a window and is controlled by a user. Select the Show Scrollbar check box if you want the scrollbar to be visible for the user. The Browsed at a Kiosk option displays a full screen show that runs automatically.

   - **Show Options:** Select the Loop Continuously until 'Esc' check box to enable the show to repeat continuously until you press Esc. Choose whether to run the show with narration and animation.

   - **Pen Color:** Select your desired pen color from the drop-down list.

   - **Show Slides:** By default, PowerPoint will display all your slides in the show. You can also specify a range of slides, if desired, by clicking the up and down arrows.

   - **Advance Slides:** See the sections "Set Timing for Slides Manually" and "Set Timings for Slides While Rehearsing" coming up in this chapter.

   - **Multiple Monitors:** You can run your presentation on more than one monitor.

   - **Performance:** See the upcoming section, "Optimizing Slide Show Performance," for details.

4. Click OK.

Figure 15-1: Specify your slide show options

Remember to always double-check all your presentation hardware before giving your presentation. If possible, be sure to rehearse your presentation with the actual hardware you will be using.

Set Timings for Slides Manually

1. Open a presentation in PowerPoint.

2. In Normal view, in the Slides tab area, select the slides you want to edit the timings for.

3. Choose Slide Show⇨Slide Transition.

4. In the Slide Transition pane, shown in Figure 15-2, under Advance slide, select the Automatically After check box, and enter the number of seconds you want the slide to remain on-screen before the next slide appears.

Set Timings for Slides While Rehearsing

1. Open the presentation that you want to rehearse.

2. Choose Slide Show⇨Rehearse Timings. Your slide show appears in what PowerPoint refers to as *rehearsal mode*, shown in Figure 15-3. The timing begins to record.

3. In the controls area in the top-left corner, click the Advance button (right-pointing arrow) when you're ready to go to the next slide. If you need to stop temporarily, click the Pause button, which is just to the right of the Advance button. You can manually enter a timing value for a particular slide in the Slide Time field just to the right of the Pause button. If you want to start over, click the Repeat button (curved arrow).

4. At the end of the show, a dialog box appears and asks you whether you want to accept the timings or start over.

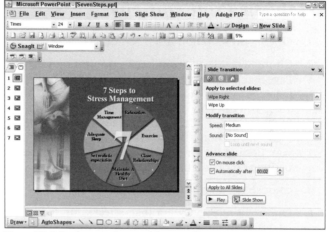

Figure 15-2: Set the timing for your slides manually
Photo Credit: Corbis Images, PhotoDisc/Getty Images

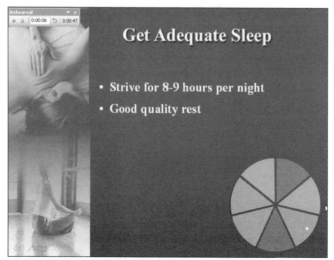

Figure 15-3: Set the timing for your slide show while rehearsing
Photo Credit: Corbis Images, PhotoDisc/Getty Images

Establish Print Options

1. Open a presentation in PowerPoint.

2. Choose File⇨Page Setup to specify print options. In the Page Setup dialog box, in the Slides Sized For drop-down list, select your output or paper size, as shown in Figure 15-4. You can choose from various paper sizes as well as 35mm slides, overhead transparencies, or a banner (8 x 1 inches). You may also enter a custom size by specifying your desired Width and Height. Specify your page numbering and orientation settings. Click OK.

3. Choose File⇨Print Preview.

4. On the Print Preview toolbar, select your desired page layout from the Print What drop-down list, as shown in Figure 15-5. Select from Slides, Handouts, Notes Pages, and Outline View. We describe each later in this chapter.

5. Still in the Print Preview Toolbar, choose your desired page orientation by selecting either the Portrait (vertical) or Landscape (horizontal) icons.

Figure 15-4: Specify your output size in the Page Setup dialog box

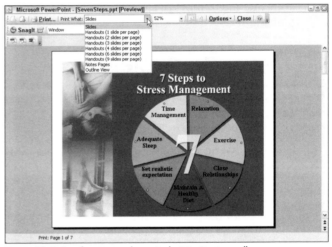

Figure 15-5: Specify your page layout in the Print Preview toolbar
Photo Credit: Corbis Images, PhotoDisc/Getty Images

6. Under the Options drop-down menu (see Figure 15-6) you find the following settings:

- **Header and Footer:** Enter your desired header and footer text in the Header and Footer dialog box. You can also choose to include the date and time in the header or footer, as shown in Figure 15-7. Check Slide number or Page number to have the number of the slide or page appear in the footer of the slide, notes page or handout. Note that headers and footers on notes pages and handouts are separate from the headers and footers on slides.

- **Color/Grayscale:** From the submenu, choose whether to print in color (be sure you've chosen a color printer), grayscale, or pure black and white. Choosing pure black and white results in no gray values in the print out.

- **Scale to Fit Paper:** If you select this option, slides will be sized to fit on your chosen paper size.

- **Frame Slides:** This option adds a frame around each printed slide.

- **Print Hidden Slides:** If you select this option, slides that you have designated to be hidden will remain hidden but will print out.

- **Print Comment and Ink Markup:** Select this option to enable reviewer comments and ink markups to print. For more on comments and ink markups, see Chapter 16.

- **Printing Order:** When printing handouts with 4, 6, or 0 slides, choose whether to print in order horizontally or vertically, as displayed by the corresponding thumbnail icon.

7. Click Print.

 Note that you can also set the preceding print options in the Print dialog box.

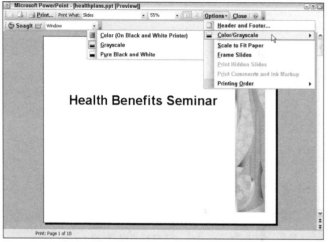

Figure 15-6: Choose additional print options

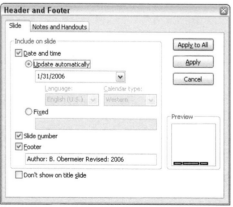

Figure 15-7: Specify header and footer options

Print Slides

1. Open a presentation in PowerPoint.

2. Choose File➪Page Setup to set up your slides for optimum printing. In the Slides Sized For drop-down list, select your paper size.

3. Choose File➪Print Preview.

4. On the Print Preview toolbar, select Slides from the Print What drop-down list, as shown in Figure 15-8.

5. Specify any additional print options as we describe in the preceding section, "Establish Print Options."

6. Click the Print button.

 Note that hidden slides with notes will print along with your other slides.

Print Audience Handouts

1. Open a presentation in PowerPoint.

2. Choose File➪Print Preview.

3. On the Print Preview toolbar, select your desired Handout layout from the Print What drop-down list, as shown in Figure 15-9. Choose 1, 2, 3, 4, 6, or 9 slides per page. Note that if you choose the 3-slide layout, blank lines will be added next to each slide to allow for audience members to take notes during the presentation.

4. Specify additional print options as we describe in the earlier section, "Establish Print Options."

5. Click the Print button.

Figure 15-8: Print your slides
Photo Credit: PhotoSpin

Figure 15-9: Print handouts for your audience

Print Speaker Notes

1. Open a presentation in PowerPoint.

2. Choose View➪Notes Page. Double-check the appearance of your notes. Format your font, font size, and so on as needed by highlighting the text and choosing Format➪ Font. You can also enlarge the slide by selecting it and dragging a corner sizing handle. You can add charts, tables, and pictures to your notes if desired. (Follow the steps that we outline in Chapters 9 and 10.) Keep in mind that any edits you make or any pictures or charts/ tables you add in Notes view will appear only on your printed notes pages, not on your screen in Normal view.

3. Choose File➪Print Preview.

4. On the Print Preview toolbar, select Notes Pages from the Print What drop-down list, as shown in Figure 15-10. Each page will print with a single slide and the associated notes for that slide. (Speaker notes are help-ful as references when delivering a presentation.)

5. Specify additional print options, as we describe in "Establish Print Options," earlier in this chapter.

6. Click the Print button.

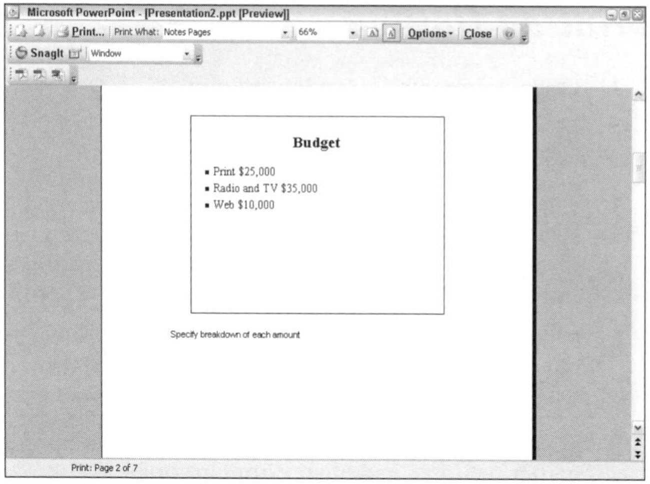

 If you want your formatting and additions of elements such as pictures and charts on all your notes pages, be sure to make the changes to the note master. For more on masters, see Chapter 6.

 Note that if you save your presentation as a Web page, your notes will be displayed by default. If you don't want them displayed, hide them before you save them. See Chapter 16 for details.

Figure 15-10: Print speaker notes

Print an Outline

1. Open a presentation in PowerPoint.

2. In Normal view, click the Outline tab next to the Slides tab, as shown in Figure 15-11.

3. Click the Expand All button on the Standard toolbar, also shown in Figure 15-11. This shows all levels of text on the slide. (If you want only slide titles to print, do not click the Expand All button.)

4. Choose File➪Print Preview. On the Print Preview toolbar, select Outline View from the Print What drop-down list, as shown in Figure 15-12.

5. Specify additional print options, as we describe in the earlier section, "Establish Print Options."

6. Click the Print button.

 You may want to print your outline to use during a slide show to keep yourself on track as to what topics are coming up as you progress through your presentation. Using an outline allows you to have an overall global view of your presentation material.

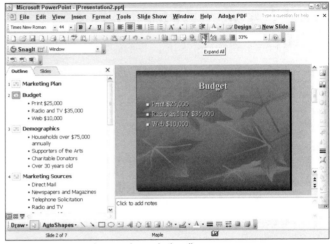

Figure 15-11: Expand your outline to display all text

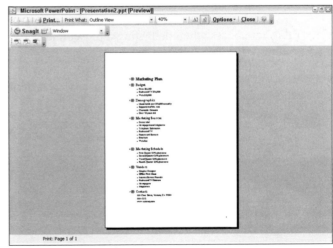

Figure 15-12: Print an outline

Send Handouts, Notes, or an Outline to Microsoft Word

1. Open a presentation in PowerPoint.

2. Choose File➪Send To➪Microsoft Office Word.

3. In the Send To Microsoft Office Word dialog box, shown in 15-13, select the desired page layout for your presentation:

- **Handouts:** Choose either Blank Lines Next to Slides or Blank Lines Below Slides.

- **Notes:** Choose Notes Next to Slides or Notes Below Slides.

- **Outline:** Choose Outline only, as shown in Figure 15-13.

 If you choose Handouts or Notes, specify whether you want to add the slides to Word as embedded files (paste) or linked files (paste link). Note that if you link the files, when you update them in PowerPoint they will also be updated in Word.

4. Click OK.

5. Your chosen presentation information will appear as a new document in Word, as shown in Figure 15-14. Edit, format, and print the information as desired.

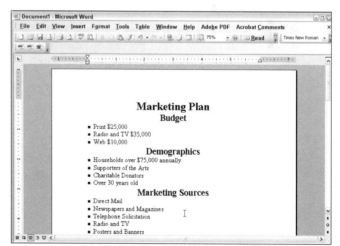

Figure 15-13: Specify what elements you want to send to Word

Figure 15-14: Edit and print your PowerPoint outline from Word
Photo Credit: PhotoSpin

Create a Backup by Packaging for CD

1. Insert a blank CD into your drive.

2. Open the presentation that you want to package.

3. Make sure your presentation is ready for packaging by reviewing all information. Remember to look at elements such as notes, comments, and ink annotations. If you don't want to include them, delete them now.

4. Choose File⇨Package for CD.

5. In the Package for CD dialog box, shown in Figure 15-15, name the CD.

6. If you want to add files that aren't automatically included in the packaging, click the Add Files button. In the Add Files dialog box that appears — shown in Figure 15-16 — navigate to and select your desired files. (Note that all linked files, along with the PowerPoint Viewer, are automatically included.) If you want to change the play order of the copied files, click the up or down arrows on the left of the dialog box. To remove a file, select it and click the Remove button. When you're done, click Add.

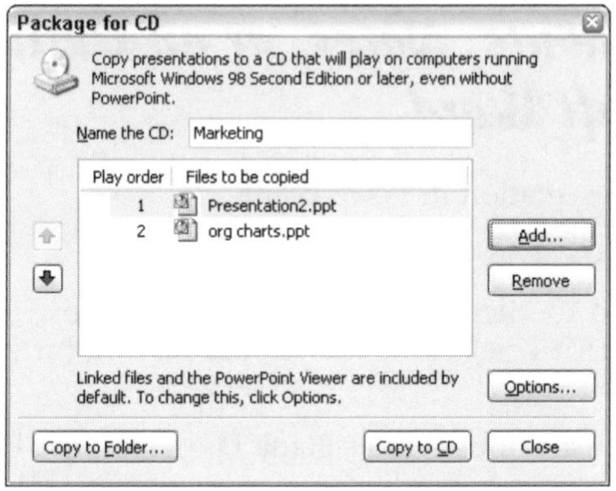

Figure 15-15: Burn a copy of your presentation onto a CD

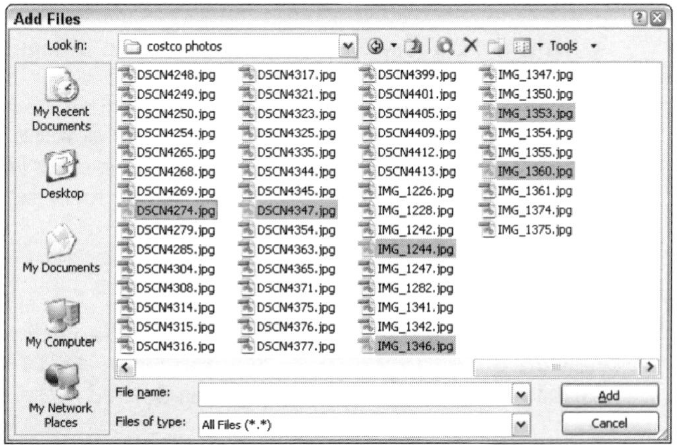

Figure 15-16: Add Files to your CD package

7. Click the Options button to specify additional settings in the Options dialog box, shown in Figure 15-17:

   • Specify whether to include the PowerPoint Viewer. The Viewer enables your presentation to play without using the PowerPoint application.

   • Specify how the presentations will play by selecting an option from the drop-down list. For example, you can enable the user to select the presentation she wants to view.

   • Choose whether to embed TrueType fonts. Note that fonts that have built-in copyright protections won't be embedded.

   • To add a password requirement for opening or modifying the presentation, type your password in the corresponding field. Note that if any of the packaged files already have passwords (for example, PDF [Portable Document Format] files), PowerPoint asks you whether you want to keep those passwords or override them.

8. Click OK to exit the Option dialog box.

9. Click Copy to CD.

 Note that the Package for CD command works only for Windows XP or later. For other operating systems, you can use the command only to copy your files to a folder. You cannot copy them directly to a CD. To burn the files onto a CD, use your default CD burning application.

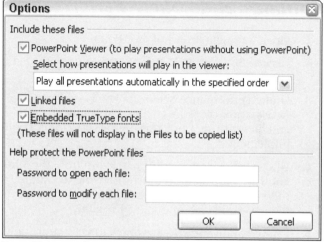

Figure 15-17: Specify your presentation CD options

 Always make a backup of your presentation onto other media, such as a USB jump drive or a CD. That way you'll be prepared if the original file on your hard drive gets corrupted or you have some kind of computer glitch.

Optimize Slide Show Performance

1. Open a presentation in PowerPoint.

2. Choose Slide Show➪Set Up Show to open the Set Up Show dialog box.

3. Under Performance, select the Use Hardware Graphics Acceleration check box, shown in Figure 15-18. If your graphics card supports this option, PowerPoint will implement it.

4. Under Performance, select 640 x 480 from the Slide Show Resolution drop-down list. Note that although this setting yields the fastest performance, it also yields the lowest fidelity, or quality. Click OK.

5. Choose Slide Show➪View Show to view your show with the edited settings. If you see any problems, go back to the default settings.

 Click the Tips button to get further information on how to improve slide show performance.

 Another thing you can do to improve the performance of the slide show is to work with your animations. Try reducing the size or your animated pictures. Also try to limit your use of animations that fade, rotate, or change size. Finally, limit your use of animated objects that include gradients or transparency.

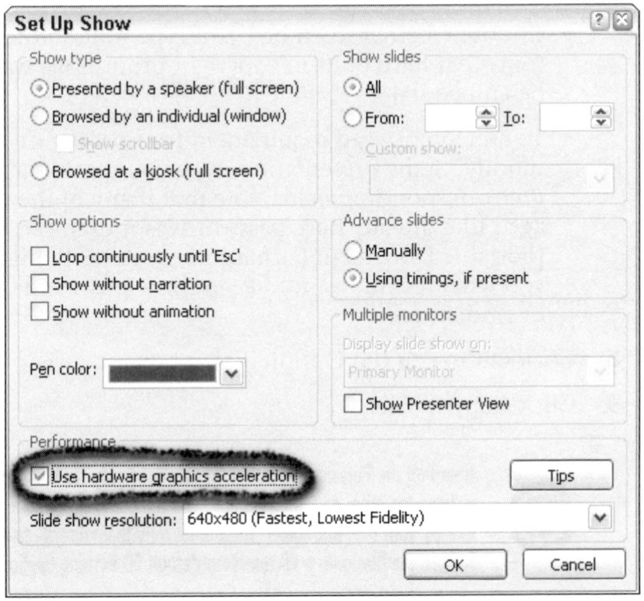

Figure 15-18: Improve your slide show performance if it appears sluggish

Sharing Your Presentation

*W*hat good is a wonderful presentation if you don't share it with the world? PowerPoint offers you many ways to share. You can take the traditional and most personal route and present the show yourself (or choose a designated live body). If you're short on manpower or want to free up people for other tasks, you can present a self-running show. If you need feedback on a presentation, PowerPoint has a great system of sending a presentation out for review. Need to collaborate? PowerPoint also provides a way, with the help of Microsoft NetMeeting, to hold online meetings. Finally, you can take the more technical route and share your presentation online via the Internet. This is a great way to disseminate information to a large audience or to people who are located in geographically diverse locations. This chapter gives you all you need to know to finalize your show and then share it with others.

Get ready to . . .

Create a Custom Show

1. Open a presentation in PowerPoint.

2. Choose Slide Show➪Custom Shows.

3. In the Custom Shows dialog box, shown in Figure 16-1, click New.

4. In the Define Custom Show dialog box, shown in Figure 16-2, select the slides you want to include in the custom show. Click Add.

5. If you need to change the order of the slides, click on the slide you want to move to select it and then click the up or down arrow buttons on the right.

6. Give your custom show a name and click OK.

7. Click Close to close the Custom Shows dialog box. Click Show to see a preview of the show. Note that you can also edit, remove, or copy your custom show by clicking the appropriate button on the right.

 A *custom show* is simply a grouping of slides within your presentation that you can present separately from your main presentation or that you can hyperlink to. This can come in handy if you need to make presentations to several different groups within an organization. For example, everyone might need to view the main presentation, but you can create custom shows to present to individual groups who have slightly different needs.

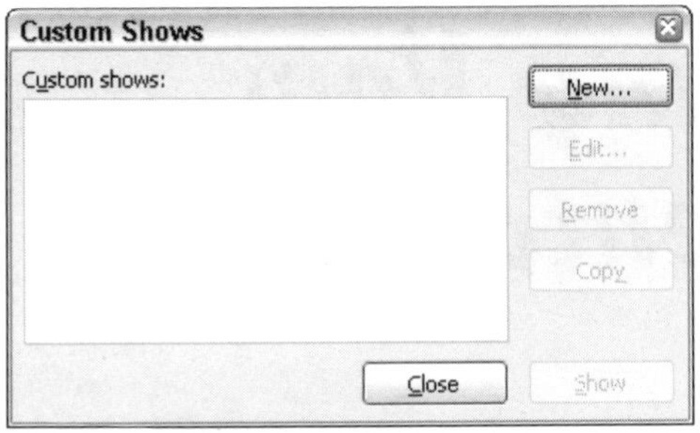

Figure 16-1: Create a custom show

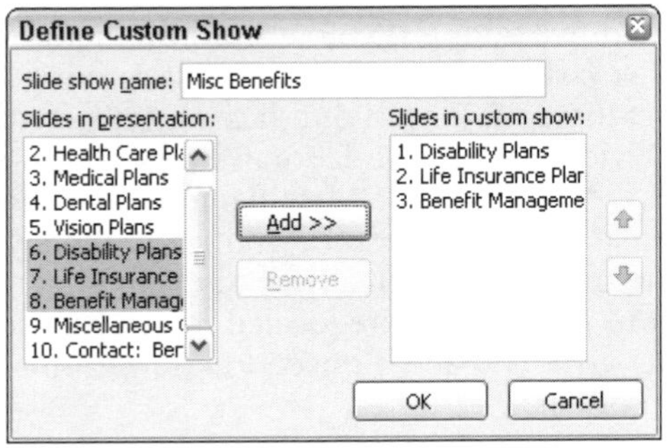

Figure 16-2: Select the slides to include in your custom show

 To present a custom show, choose Slide Show➪Set Up Show. Under Show slides, select Custom Show and select your desired show from the drop-down list. Click OK. Then simply choose Slide Show➪View Show.

 For details on hyperlinking to your custom show, see Chapter 13.

Prepare a Self-Directed Show

1. Open the presentation in PowerPoint. You can simply choose Slide Show➪View Show or click the Slide Show button in the bottom-left corner of the application window. If you want to specify further options, proceed to Step 2.

2. Choose Slide Show➪Set Up Show.

3. In the Set Up Show dialog box, as shown in Figure 16-3, choose the Presented by a Speaker (Full Screen) option. Specify your other options:

   • **Show Options:** Select the Loop Continuously until 'Esc' option to enable the show to repeat continuously until you press Esc. This is usually selected when preparing a show for a kiosk. Choose whether to run the show with narration and animation.

   • **Pen color:** Select your desired pen color from the drop-down list. You can make notes on your slides during a presentation (see the Tip following this step list).

   • **Show Slides:** By default, PowerPoint displays all the slides in the show. You can also specify a range of slides, if desired, by clicking the up and down arrows. If your presentation contains a custom show, you may also select it from the Custom Show drop-down list.

   • **Advance Slides:** See Chapter 15 for more details.

   • **Multiple Monitors:** You can run your presentation on more than one monitor. See the section "Use Two Monitors to Run a Presentation," later in this chapter.

   • **Performance:** See the section on optimizing slide show performance in Chapter 15 for details.

 You can write on your slides during a presentation by using the PowerPoint pen. During your slide show, right-click and choose Pointer Option from the contextual menu. Select a pen type from the submenu. Press and drag your mouse to create a pen mark, as shown in Figure 16-4.

Figure 16-3: Specify options for your self-directed show

Figure 16-4: Use the PowerPoint pen to emphasize important points

Use a Laptop and Projector to Run Your Show

1. Using the cable that shipped with the projector, connect the external display port on the laptop to the projector. Additionally, if you'll be using an audio cable to add sound, connect the audio port on your laptop to the projector.

2. Set the resolution of your laptop display to match that of the projector. In Windows, choose Start⇨Settings⇨ Control Panel. In the Control Panel window, click Display.

3. In the Display Properties dialog box, click the Settings tab. In the Settings dialog box, shown in Figure 16-5, set your desired resolution under Screen Resolution. If you are unsure what resolution to use, set it to 800 x 600 pixels.

4. Click OK to close the Display Properties dialog box.

Use Two Monitors to Run a Presentation

1. Choose Slide Show⇨Set Up Show.

2. In the Set Up Show dialog box, shown in Figure 16-6, under Multiple Monitors, select the monitor you want your slide show to appear on.

3. Select the Show Presenter View check box to enable you to run your presentation in presenter mode.

4. Click OK to close the Display Properties dialog box.

Using two monitors enables you to run your presentation from one monitor while displaying your presentation to your audience on another. This allows you to have other applications open that your audience can't see. You can also use presenter view, which gives you access to additional tools in your presentation, such as showing slides out of order and blacking out the screen on your audience's monitor.

Figure 16-5: Match the laptop display's resolution to your projector

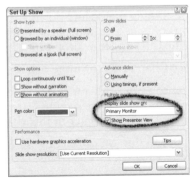

Figure 16-6: Run your presentation by using a primary and secondary monitor

Set Permissions

1. Open a presentation in PowerPoint.

2. Choose File⇨Permission⇨Do Not Distribute. You can also click the Permission button on the Standard toolbar.

3. The Microsoft Office dialog box explains the Information Rights Management feature. Click Yes if you need to install the latest version of Windows Rights Management client. Click No if you already have it.

4. In the Permission dialog box, shown in Figure 16-7, select the Restrict Permission to This Presentation option.

5. In the Read and Change fields, type the names or e-mail addresses of your recipients.

6. Click More Options for additional settings. The additional settings are fairly self-explanatory, as shown in Figure 16-8. For example, you can enter an expiration date for the presentation. You can also include an e-mail address so that users can request further permissions. And, you can require users to connect to the Internet to verify their permission prior to viewing the presentation. Click the Set Defaults button to make your settings the default settings for permissions. Click OK.

7. Click OK to close the Permission dialog box.

 You can set permissions only in PowerPoint 2003. Previous editions do not support this feature. You must also install the latest version of the Windows Rights Management client.

 To view the permissions you have for a presentation, choose View⇨ Task Pane. Select Shared Workspace from the Task Pane drop-down list. Click the Status tab to view the permissions.

 To remove permissions, choose File⇨Permission⇨Unrestricted Access.

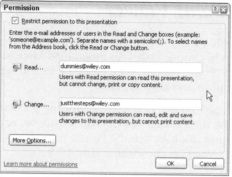

Figure 16-7: Set permissions for your presentation

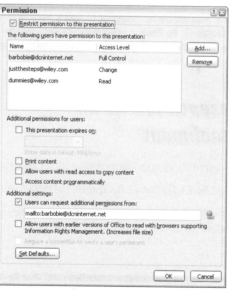

Figure 16-8: Specify additional permission's options

Use PowerPoint Viewer

1. If you downloaded and installed PowerPoint Viewer from the Web, choose Start➪All Programs➪Microsoft Office PowerPoint Viewer 2003. Navigate to and select the presentation and click Open.

2. If you packaged PowerPoint viewer with the presentation by using the Package for CD command, navigate to that folder and double-click the PowerPoint viewer file (`pptview.exe`), as shown in Figure 16-9.

 PowerPoint Viewer is an application that enables you to run presentations without having PowerPoint installed. You must have PowerPoint Viewer installed on your computer before you or your recipients can use it. When you use the Package for CD feature, which we describe in Chapter 12, the Viewer is automatically installed. Otherwise you can download it free of charge from Microsoft Office Online at `http://office.microsoft.com`.

Send a Presentation as an E-Mail Attachment

1. Open the presentation you want to save as an attachment.

2. Choose File➪Send To➪Mail Recipient (as Attachment).

3. In the To and Cc fields, enter the e-mail addresses of your recipients, as shown in Figure 16-10.

4. Click Send.

 If you want your presentation to automatically start when the recipient opens the attachment, save it as a PowerPoint Show with a `.pps` extension.

 If your recipient doesn't have PowerPoint, instruct her in the e-mail message to download the Microsoft Office PowerPoint 2003 Viewer from `www.microsoft.com`.

Figure 16-9: View a presentation with PowerPoint Viewer

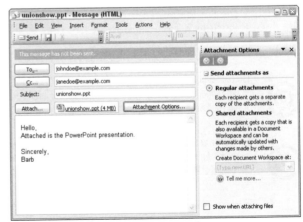

Figure 16-10: Send your presentation via e-mail

Send a Presentation for Review

1. Open the presentation you want to have reviewed in PowerPoint. Make sure you have included all linked files in one of the following items, depending on your review method: your e-mail message; a regular folder; a shared folder (for sending via a network server); or a disk (for sending via disks). Alternatively, make sure to embed your linked files within the presentation.

2. If you're using Microsoft Outlook, choose File⇨Send To⇨Mail Recipient (for Review). In the To and Cc fields, enter the e-mail addresses of your recipients. Click Send and you're done. Skip the rest of this step list.

3. If you're using another mail client, a network server, or disks, choose File⇨Save As. In the Save As dialog box, shown in Figure 16-11, name your presentation. We recommend putting a number, letter, or the reviewer's name after the presentation name. Select Presentation for Review from the Save as Type drop-down list. Click Save. Proceed to Step 4.

4. If you're using an e-mail client or Web mail, simply attach the presentation and linked files as normal e-mail attachments, shown in Figure 16-12. If you're using a network server, gather all your reviewer presentations into a shared folder on the network server. If you're sending out disks, copy each reviewer's presentation and linked files to disks and send them out.

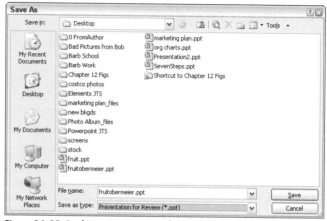

Figure 16-11: Send your presentation out for review

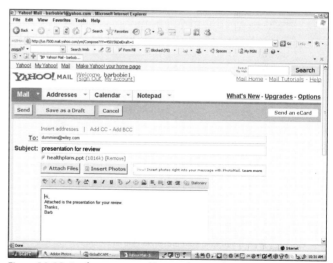

Figure 16-12: Attach a presentation like any other e-mail attachment

Review a Presentation

1. To review a presentation, double-click to open the attachment.

2. Make any necessary changes while reviewing the presentation in PowerPoint.

3. To add a comment, choose Insert⇨Comment. Type the comment and click outside the comment box. Comments are designated by an icon on the slide, as shown in Figure 16-13.

3. When you're done, if you received it through Microsoft Outlook, choose File⇨Send To⇨Original Sender. If you want to edit the message before sending the reviewed presentation back, click Reply with Changes on the Reviewing toolbar.

4. If you received it from another mail client or via a network server or disk, choose File⇨Save and return the presentation to the original sender via your desired method.

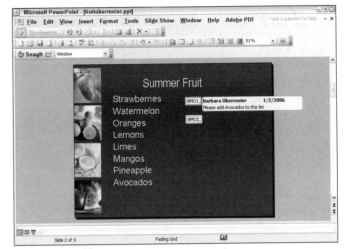

Figure 16-13: Add review comments to your presentation

Combine Reviewed Presentations with the Original

1. If you're using Microsoft Outlook, double-click the reviewed presentation attachment.

2. In the alert dialog box, click Yes to combine the reviewed presentation with your original. Repeat Steps 1 and 2 as necessary.

3. If you're using another mail client, a network server, or disks, open your original presentation.

4. Select Tools⇨Compare and Merge Presentations.

5. In the Choose Files to Merge with Current Presentation dialog box, shown in Figure 16-14, select the reviewed presentations that you want to combine with your original. Click Merge.

6. Your reviewed presentations are combined with your original. Revisions will be annotated by a marker, along with the actual revisions, as shown in Figure 16-15. The Revisions pane will also list the revisions.

 You can combine reviewers' presentations with your original presentation so that you can view all changes and comments simultaneously.

 To end a review so that no further combining can be done, click the End Review button on the Reviewing toolbar.

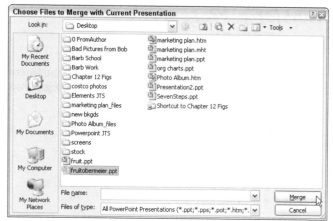

Figure 16-14: Combine your reviewed presentations into one

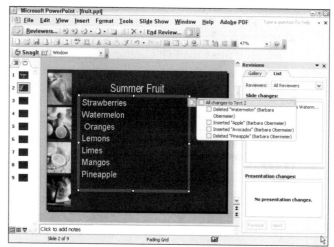

Figure 16-15: Reviewers' comments will be annotated by a marker

Transfer a Presentation to an FTP Site

1. Make sure your computer is connected to the Internet and you have the proper FTP address and login and password information handy.

2. Open your presentation in PowerPoint.

3. Select File⇨Save As.

4. In the Save As dialog box, shown in Figure 16-16, click the Save In arrow to access the drop-down list. Do one of the following:

   - If you don't have the FTP address set up yet, select Add/Modify FTP Locations. In the dialog box, shown in Figure 16-17, enter the FTP site name, login name, and password.

   - If you have FTP addresses set up, select your desired location from the FTP Locations folder.

5. When the FTP site is accessed, navigate to the folder on the FTP server where you will be storing your presentation. Click Save.

 If your file is very large, saving it to an FTP site is a good way to transfer your file.

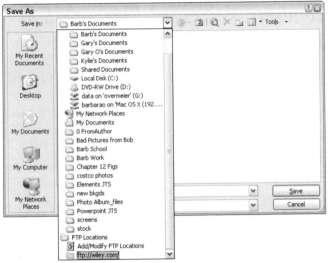

Figure 16-16: Save your presentation to an FTP site

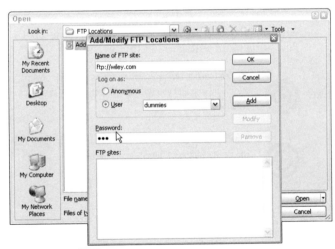

Figure 16-17: Add FTP sites

Convert a Presentation to PDF

1. Open your presentation in PowerPoint.

2. If you have Adobe Acrobat installed, choose Adobe PDF⇨Convert to Adobe PDF, as shown in Figure 16-18.

3. In the Save Adobe PDF File As dialog box, navigate to the location where you want to save your file. Give the file a name. Your file type should be PDF.

4. Click Save. Your presentation is converted to a PDF.

 You cannot convert a presentation directly to PDF from PowerPoint; you have to use a third-party application. Adobe Acrobat (the full version) is the program of choice. When you install Acrobat, it automatically installs a PDF Maker add-in to PowerPoint, which becomes part of your menu bar, as shown in Figure 16-18. Many other less expensive programs are also available, such as PDF Creator, GhostScript/ Ghost View, and so on.

Create a Self-Running Presentation for a Booth or Kiosk

1. Open the presentation in PowerPoint.

2. Select Slide Show⇨Set Up Show.

3. In the Set Up Show dialog box, as shown in Figure 16-19, select the Browsed at a Kiosk (Full Screen) option. Be sure to add automatic timings so that the slides advance automatically. If you want users to control the show, add action buttons so they may click to advance the slides. (For more on action buttons, see Chapter 11.)

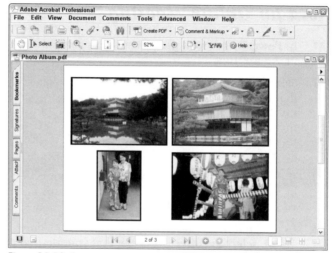

Figure 16-18: Convert your presentation to a PDF by using a third-party application

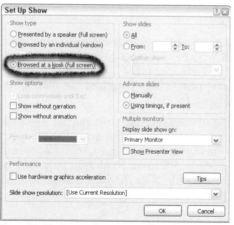

Figure 16-19: Create a show to run itself at a kiosk

Hold an Online Meeting

1. In PowerPoint, open the presentation you want to use in the meeting.

2. Select Tools⇨Online Collaboration⇨Meet Now. Note that to participate in an online meeting participants must have Microsoft Windows NetMeeting running on their computers. They must also be logged in to a directory server. If you've used NetMeeting before, proceed to Step 4.

3. If this is the first time you've used NetMeeting, you will be presented with the NetMeeting dialog box. Enter your information. Click OK.

4. In the Find Someone dialog box, shown in Figure 16-20, select the directory server that your desired participants are logged in to from the Select a Directory drop-down list. Select a participant's name from the list. Click Call. Repeat this process for all of your desired participants.

5. Click Close to close the Find Someone dialog box. Any participants who have accepted the meeting request will appear in the Participants list on the Online Meeting toolbar that appears when you close the dialog box, as shown in Figure 16-21.

6. To send a file to your meeting participants, select File⇨Send To⇨Online Meeting Participant. All participants will receive the file in their `ProgramFiles\NetMeeting\ Received Files` folders. To prevent participants from changing a shared file, click the Stop Others from Editing button on the Online Meeting toolbar.

7. To end a meeting, the host can click the End Meeting button on the Online Meeting toolbar.

To chat with meeting participants, the host can click the Display Chat Window button on the Online Meeting toolbar.

Figure 16-20: Select your meeting participants in the Find Someone dialog box

Figure 16-21: Control the meeting with the Online Meeting toolbar

Deliver a Presentation on the Web

1. Open the presentation you want to publish to the Web in PowerPoint.

2. Select File⇨Save as Web Page.

3. In the Save As dialog box, as shown in Figure 16-22, enter a filename and select your file type as follows:

   • **Web Page:** Saves the presentation as a Web page and then creates a folder with supporting elements.

   • **Single File Web Page:** Saves the presentation as a Web page with all supporting elements integrated into that page.

4. To change the title of your Web page, click the Change Title button. Enter your title in the Set Page Title dialog box. This title will appear in the title bar of the browser.

5. Click Publish. In the Publish as Web Page dialog box, shown in Figure 16-23, set your options as follows:

   • **Publish What:** Choose from Complete Presentation or a range of slides. Choose whether to display any speaker notes.

   • **Web Options:** Click this button to access additional options for animations, font support, and so on.

   • **Browser Support:** Select a browser version.

   • **Publish a Copy As:** Leave the title of your Web page as is or click Change to type in a new title. Click the Browse button to navigate to the location where you want to save your page. In the Publish As dialog box, you can also type a different filename. Click OK.

   • **Open Published Web Page in Browser:** Select this option to have your Web page open in your specified browser.

6. Click Publish. Your presentation is now Web ready.

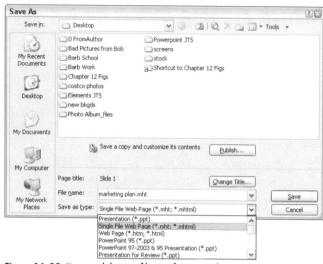

Figure 16-22: Name and choose a file type for your Web page

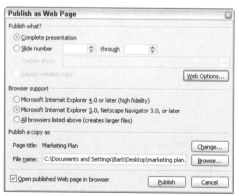

Figure 16-23: Specify your Web page options

Publish a Photo Album on the Web

1. Open a presentation in PowerPoint.

2. Select File⇨Save as Web Page.

3. In the Save As dialog box, click Publish.

4. In the Publish as Web Page dialog box, specify your desired options, which we describe in the preceding section, "Deliver a Presentation on the Web."

5. Click Publish. Your photo album is now available for viewing on the Web, as shown in Figure 16-24.

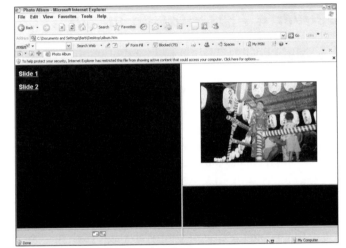

Figure 16-24: Photo album viewed in a browser

Index

• P •